SPEED READING

SPEED READING

ROBERT L. ZORN, Ph.D.

Harper Perennial
A Division of HarperCollins*Publishers*

Library of Congress Cataloging-in-Publication Data

Zorn, Robert L.
    Speed reading / Robert L. Zorn. — Rev. ed., 1st Harper Perennial ed.
        p.   cm.
    Includes index.
    ISBN 0-06-463734-4
    1. Rapid reading.   I. Title.
LB1050.54.Z67   1991
428.4'3—dc20   90-39179

92 93 94 95 CG/MPC 10 9 8 7 6 5 4 3 2

To my wife, Joan

CONTENTS

SPEED READING

Chapter 1

GETTING STARTED

For many people, getting started is the major obstacle to reading faster. You've already taken the first step. This book unlocks the basic secrets of speed reading. It presents the key steps to faster and better reading. These procedures have worked each year for thousands of people who have doubled or tripled their reading speed in classes I have taught at various schools, colleges, and universities. The methods presented here are the same successful techniques that have worked for many people for many years. With this book to help you, you're on your way to reading better and faster.

One of the first questions most people have when becoming involved in the art of speed reading is: "How does my present reading speed compare to that of others?"

To answer this question, you need to know two things at the outset: your reading speed and your level of comprehension—the two major facets of the reading process. Determining your normal reading rate and your average level of comprehension is an ideal starting point on the road to better, more enjoyable reading. You can use this information as a basis for comparison with other people and, more importantly, as a basis for measuring your improvement and progress throughout this book.

In order to ascertain your reading rate and comprehension level, read the following paragraph and time in seconds how long it takes you to read the entire paragraph. It is important that you read in a comfortable manner that reflects your average or normal rate. Do not try to go excessively fast or slow. Remember: The purpose is to find your usual reading rate. A stopwatch would be ideal to time your reading, but any clock or watch that enables you to keep track of the seconds will do fine. Just record *in seconds* how long it takes you to read this one paragraph at your normal rate.

All set? Begin.

Reading #1

OUR UNTAPPED READING POTENTIAL

Very few people make full use of the abilities they have as far as reading is concerned. Figures from research indica te that we use only 15 percent of our available mental resources when we are engaged in recognizing symbols, recalling their meanings, and then assembling those meanings into some resemblance of what the writer had in mind. We would take our car to the nearest garage at once if it were not performing smoothly and efficiently. Yet we don't give our reading abilities the same consideration. Once our reading skill is properly developed, it needs only consistent and proper use to keep it in the very best condition.

How many seconds did it take you? Record your time for this first reading on the Progress Chart in the back of the book (page 149), beside Reading #1, under the heading "seconds."

This chart will enable you to keep an accurate record of your progress.

Next convert the seconds it took you to read that paragraph into words per minute (WPM)—your reading rate or speed—by using the following chart. Remember, this should reflect your comfortable or normal reading rate on this paragraph:

Time/Sec	10	15	20	25	30	35	40	45	50	60
WPM	780	472	354	283	236	202	177	157	141	118

If the number of seconds it took you to read the paragraph isn't shown on the chart above, divide the number of seconds it took you to read the paragraph into 7080. This will give you your exact WPM. Next, place your WPM score for Reading #1 in the column headed "WPM" on the Progress Chart on page 149.

Now we want to find your comprehension level for reading the paragraph. The following is a comprehension quiz. Don't refer back to the paragraph. If you don't know the answer or can't remember, just take a guess. There's no penalty for guessing on these questions. Remember, the idea here is simply to find some basic indication of your comprehension skills.

Place your answers on the line provided after each statement. Use the following symbols for your answers: True (T), False (F), or Not Mentioned (N). The tricky part here is the (N) for Not Mentioned. It forces the reader to remember if the topic or point in question was *specifically mentioned* in the paragraph. It also reduces the guessing factor that would occur in a true-false quiz, in which the student has a fifty-fifty chance of guessing the right answer. The insertion of "Not Mentioned" thus enables you to have a more accurate idea of what your comprehension level really is. Let's try this comprehension quiz.

1. Few people make full use of their ability when they read.
   T

2. The task of recognizing symbols and recalling meanings takes much energy. _____

3. We spend more money on our cars than we spend on our reading skills. _____

4. We should take better care of our reading skills. _____

5. Reading skill, like a car, needs to be overhauled at regular intervals. _____

To find your comprehension score, refer to "Answers to Reading Exercises," on page 151.

Give yourself 20 points for each right answer on this comprehension quiz and record your score for Reading #1 in the "comprehension" column on the Progress Chart (page 149).

Your score is a percentage of accuracy that indicates your comprehension level. You have now completed the following: You read the first exercise and timed how long it took in seconds; you found your WPM; you took a quiz and discovered your comprehension level. The steps you've just completed are the hardest exercises required in this book. From here on, everything gets easier and easier.

The next thing to do is to compare the results of your speed and comprehension scores on this first reading to those achieved on the same material by people of similar educational levels (see the chart on page 5). The average adult usually reads this paragraph at the rate of approximately 200 WPM. The average high-school student reads it at the rate of about 250 WPM, the average college student at about 325 WPM. A student in graduate school would read it at about 400 WPM.

One statistic shown on the chart opposite may surprise you: the average reading rate for adults.

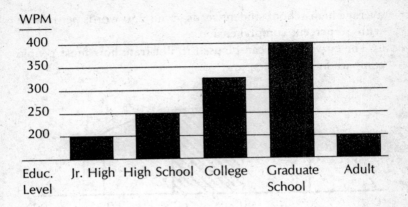

The reason most adults read at 200 WPM, even if they are college graduates, is quite simple: The amount of reading they do (once they leave school) is not anywhere near the volume they read when they were students. Therefore, their reading speed has gradually tapered off and leveled out to a rate of 200 WPM.

An individual's reading speed varies somewhat, about 25 WPM above or below the base reading rate shown on the chart. You can add or subtract 25 WPM from your score and see what it does to your reading rate in comparison with the norm shown on the chart.

Keep these figures in mind as you set a goal for yourself. How fast do you wish to read? *You should be able to double or triple your reading rate,* at the same time maintaining or improving your comprehension.

We're now ready to examine the second major facet of reading—comprehension. The average person usually comprehends only about 50 percent of what he or she reads. In other words, we could make the following general statements: The average adult reads 200 WPM and comprehends about 50 percent of what he or she is reading. The average college student reads 325 WPM and comprehends approximately 50 percent. The average high-school student reads about 250 words per minute with 50 percent comprehension.

The curve below can be used to illustrate how most people compare in comprehension:

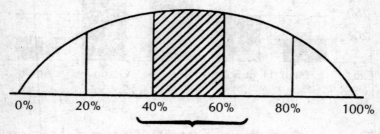

50% Comprehension (Most People)

By now you should have a good understanding of your reading abilities in both speed and comprehension. You should also have a good idea of how you compare to others. You can significantly improve both of these skills if you want to. You can become whatever kind of reader you want to be. It is not uncommon for high-school pupils, college students, and adults to increase their reading rate by 50 or 100 percent in a relatively short time, while at the same time maintaining or even increasing their comprehension!

There are many myths and false conceptions about speed-reading, such as:

Fast readers are inaccurate readers. Slow readers make up for their plodding along by getting more out of their reading. Fast readers miss everything.
Slow readers can't be expected to improve since they weren't taught to read quickly.

All of these statements are false. This book contains proven steps that will show you how to succeed in achieving new reading skills.

You might say, "OK, I can improve. You've convinced me. But how long will it take and exactly what am I supposed to do?" The simple test of your reading speed and comprehension that you have just completed gives you some insight into the answer, by showing you how your reading skills compare to those of other people. Part of the answer also hinges on your answer to a key question: How much do you want to improve? At what level or rate will you be satisfied with your reading?

You will see improvement with every step you take. Some improvement can be seen in minutes! You've already taken the most important step just by reading this chapter. This book has already started you on a program to replace old reading habits with new, faster, and better reading techniques. If you are willing to practice a little as you read each day, you will be amazed at the improvement and change in your reading skills.

What about permanent improvement? If you introduce these steps into your everyday reading habits, you will trade in your old reading skills for new ones and overhaul your reading style—permanently! There's no need for continued periodic practice or an annual retest. Speed reading is like using a muscle: To keep it in shape, all you have to do is use it. As long as you use your new reading skills, you'll never revert to the old style of slow, cumbersome reading. You will read better and faster.

Chapter 2

YOU'RE ON YOUR WAY!

Let's quickly review your progress so far. You now know your reading speed and have a good idea of your comprehension level. You know how you compare to others who have a similar educational background. You have set a goal in terms of how fast you want to read. You have demonstrated the desire to improve. Now let's put it all together and increase your reading skills.

THEORIES ON SPEED READING

There are many theories about how to improve reading rate and comprehension level. Since all reading is dependent upon eye movements, the technique that has proven the most successful for most people is to change the basic eye movements they make in reading. In other words, the easiest method of improvement is to make the eye motions or patterns more efficient. How can this be best done? This book shows you step-by-step methods to improve your eye movements over the thousands of words you read every day.

The book does not delve into other theories on reading, such as the use of motivation or vocabulary techniques, because these methods in most instances have not achieved the desired results. For instance, there is a theory based on the rationale that a person will read faster if he or she is more interested in the material. I have found over many years of teaching reading that this is not always true. People often read slower when they like what they are reading, because they tend to savor each word or each line or each paragraph. On the other hand, some people do read faster when they read material they're deeply interested in. They become engrossed in what they're reading and the words begin to fly by. However, since some people read slower and some read faster when reading interesting material, this obviously isn't the best basis on which to improve your reading rate. It's too unpredictable and varies too much from person to person and from topic to topic.

Then there's the vocabulary method. This approach is based on the belief that when people build or expand their vocabulary then and only then will they read faster. But how could that be, when most people know most of the words they read every day and yet don't read any faster? Once you're an adult, you know most of the words you see in ordinary reading matter. Even students in high school and college know most of the words they see everyday. The fact that we periodically encounter new words does not negate our whole approach to reading speed and comprehension.

Another popular theory is that the eye will follow a moving object. Therefore all you need to do is to move an object such as your finger, a pencil, or a ruler up and down the page at a fast clip and your eyes will follow accordingly—and you will soon be speed reading.

It is true that the eye will follow an object that moves across its path of vision, but who wants to depend on moving a finger or a pencil up and down the page in order to read faster? Those who like this method argue that you use these devices only in the beginning. Once you learn to read faster, you don't need them to keep your eyes moving rapidly across the printed page. But this isn't always the case because sometimes these techniques become habit-forming.

Another aspect of this technique is that people using it usually become accustomed to moving their fingers or other guides at a certain speed or rate. That rate is controlled by the mind because the mind controls the finger. Thus the reading rate is still controlled by the eye-mind relationship and eye movements.

Why not sidestep that whole debate and use a much easier method? What you want is to improve your reading so that you have the flexibility to read fast when you want to and to understand what you are reading. You wish to achieve this goal without taking a course in vocabulary building or being forced to read certain kinds of simple material so that you will read faster simply because it is easy. You don't want to rely on moving your fingers up and down a page in order to read faster.

This isn't to say these theories are all wrong, but years of experience in teaching people of all age levels, and of varied backgrounds and education, have taught me what methods work for most people and what methods are the easiest to master. These concepts are presented for you in this book, along with practical exercises, so that you can immediately apply the new concepts of speed reading and actually see your progress.

Putting all these other theories aside, let us now look at the first secret to faster reading—improving your eye movement patterns. Good and bad eye movements, or patterns, are the result of our everyday reading habits. Very few schools teach eye movements, which in most cases evolve or happen naturally as a person learns to read. Very often, bad eye-movement habits are easily developed and, if not corrected, they make us read slowly and ineffectively. Efficient eye movements must be learned, and that's what this book is all about.

REGRESSIONS

One of the habits that slows down most readers is called *regression*. This is simply backward eye movement or reading a word over again. Regressions are back-up, or reverse, motions of the eyes, and are unnecessary and inefficient. They actually intrude on the logical sequence of the material you are reading. Some reading experts claim that *regression is the most wasteful step in the average person's everyday reading activities*. This claim is just the opposite of what is often believed about reading, for many people have told me they had thought regressions improved their comprehension and speed—until they took my course. Then they found that as soon as they eliminated most of their regressions, their speed and comprehension began to increase. Many readers double their reading speed when they eliminate or reduce regressions.

Good readers glance back occasionally, but their regressions are few and far between. Let me put it this way: If you're after speed, you're not going to get it by going backward. Speed readers go forward at rapid rates with very few or no backward eye movements.

There are two types of regressions. *Involuntary regression* is a habit from earlier years of reading. *Voluntary regression* is done under the controlled awareness of the reader to clarify a crucial point in the reading selection. The latter type of regression is occasionally needed, but it should be used very sparingly.

Here is an example designed to show how both reading speed and comprehension are hindered by regressions:

Look at this sentence: This house is for sale. It contains

words every adult knows. Here's how a fast reader would move his or her eyes over this sentence in one easy, fast movement:

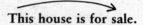

This house is for sale.

There are no hesitations, no backward eye movements, no insertion of re-read words into the sentence structure.

However, if a reader were to regress on the word "house," this insertion into the sequential pattern or flow of words being sent to the brain is confusing. Here's the pattern of eye movements when a reader regresses on the word "house":

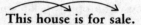

This house is for sale.

Here's the sequence of words coming into the brain when a reader regresses on the word "house":

This house is house is for sale.

Confusing? You bet it is. Regression not only causes a loss of comprehension or understanding, it really kills reading speed. That is why many people double or triple their reading speed and simultaneously improve their comprehension when they eliminate or control regressions in their daily reading.

Imagine regressing once on every line. Think how that would impede progress. Some readers in my classes have had two or more regressions on every line they read. Each regression "costs" 50 WPM in lost time. With the sentence "This house is for sale," there is no excuse for regression because the words are all known.

Once learned, reading is a skill we put on instant replay

whenever we need it. Regression—going back over the letters and words as we stumble along—are necessary when we are first learning to read. But after that, regressions should be controlled and not made at random or from habit. They should be made sparingly and purposefully—in other words, only when absolutely necessary. You can eliminate or greatly reduce the number of regressions simply by having an awareness or desire to reduce the regression habit.

If you don't want to rely on awareness or on trusting the eyes to self-correct this habit, you can use a 3 × 5 index card with a *reading window* cut out of it. To make a reading-window card, measure a rectangle 2½ inches long by ¼ inch high on a file card; then cut out the rectangle. A sample reading-window card looks like this:

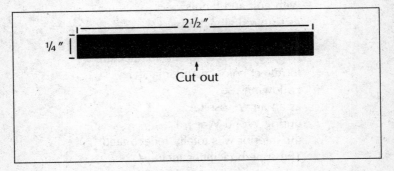

After you've made the card, place it over the following columns. Move the card down the columns. Do you see how it prevents you from regressing? Do not permit yourself to move the card up or backward at any time. Continue to move the card down until you have read the entire column. Several tries may be necessary until you get the hang of this technique. Try it. It works!

Throughout the nineteenth century
the Greenbrier was

"the" southern summer resort.
Guests came to use
the mineral water,
to enjoy the mountain climate,
and to mingle
with the famous of the day.
Today many of the original cottages
are faithfully preserved
as guest accommodations,
although enlarged and modernized.
In 1913 the central Georgian section
of the Greenbrier
opened on a
year-round basis,
with golf and tennis
as featured attractions.
Subsequent additions
have refined the hotel's architecture
to reflect colonial Virginia style.
Following use
as an army hospital
during World War I,
the interior was totally redecorated.
The superb facilities include
an exhibit hall, a conference center,
and the finest
in amenities and services
in historic hotels
of America.

Now answer the following questions about what you've just read. Just underline the correct answer.

1. The Greenbrier is: (a) a famous southern resort, (b) an historic New England hotel, (c) a Caribbean island getaway.

2. People came to the Greenbrier to: (a) mingle with the famous of the day, (b) use the mineral water, (c) enjoy the mountain climate, (d) all of the above.

Now go back and find the answers in the column you've just read. How well did you read without regressions? Try this exercise several times. You'll soon see how easy it becomes. Apply this type of drill or activity to other reading selections of your own choosing by using the reading-window card with a book or magazine you're reading. Just move it along the line of print as you read. Soon you will learn that, contrary to what many people believe, regressing does not guarantee better comprehension. After a while, you can discard usage of the window card because you will have broken yourself of the regression habit.

Regressions have serious effects on reading speed. I said earlier that every regression a reader makes, whether voluntary or involuntary, slows him or her down because every regression takes approximately 50 WPM out of the rate of speed. Now let's examine the effects of regression during a prolonged reading session. If a reader read for two hours and had only one regression per minute, just look at what would happen:

$$
\begin{array}{r}
120 \text{ minutes of reading} \\
\times\ 1 \text{ regression per minute} \\
\hline
120 \text{ regressions}
\end{array}
$$

120 regressions × 50 WPM = 6000 words
(50 WPM is what it costs the reader for each regression)

Then, 6000 divided by 200 WPM (the rate of the average reader) equals 30 minutes spent regressing out of two hours of reading.

Therefore, this reader spent 25 percent of his or her time going backward! And this was with only one regression per minute. Just think if the reader made two per minute. Then 50 percent of his or her time would be spent going backward! By now it should be obvious that you cannot read fast if regressions play a large part in your reading style.

Becoming aware of and eliminating the unnecessary eye movement called regression is critical. For the next day or two, try reading without backing up and reading words over again. See what a difference it will make. Remember that regressions for the most part are a carryover habit from the days when we first learned how to read. One point that I cannot overemphasize is that speed readers seldom regress. This is not to say they eliminate regressions absolutely; rather, they control these backward movements so that they are few and far between. In essence, regressions do three things to the reading: (1) they slow down the reading rate, (2) they cause eye fatigue, and (3) they hinder comprehension.

Now let's put theory into practice. Read the following two paragraphs, and remember: No regressions! Use the same procedure as in the first chapter: Record your time in seconds for Reading #2 on the Progress Chart on page 149. Watch how much improvement you will see compared to the first reading. You should be reading much faster already. Read each paragraph straight through. Give your reading a boost of speed!

Reading #2

INSIGHT INTO REGRESSIONS

Some of the eye movements utilized in reading are actually unnecessary. One such type of movement is called a regression. This occurs when the eyes return along the line of type being read to look again at a word or words that were already seen. This movement might be considered wasteful and time-consuming and without apparent value. However, some regressions are evident even in the best readers, so they should not be viewed as totally undesirable. It is obvious to anyone who gives it much thought, however, that if it were possible to cut down on useless eye movements, reading speed and comprehension would both be improved.

Mark the following statements either True (T), False (F), or Not Mentioned (N). Place your answers on the line after each statement.

1. Most eye movements made in reading are not necessary. _____

2. Regressions occur when the reader's vocabulary is inadequate. _____

3. Poor readers are likely to regress more often than good readers. _____

4. Reading would be improved by cutting down on useless eye movement. _____

5. Regressions might be considered as wasteful and without apparent value. _____

Time/Sec.	7	10	15	20	25	30	35	40	45	50
WPM	986	690	460	345	276	230	197	172	153	138

If your time isn't shown above, divide the number of seconds it took you to read the paragraph into 6900. This will give you your exact WPM. (For answers, see page 151). Now write your WPM and comprehension scores on the Progress Chart page 149. Now let's try another paragraph. Remember: *No regressions! None!*

Reading #3

MORE ABOUT REGRESSIONS

The need for occasional regressions in reading is a matter of a great deal of controversy. Some say one must not regress under any circumstances, while others say that a regression for the purpose of clarifying the meaning of a particular statement is not only acceptable, but may be essential if a high degree of comprehension is to be attained. There appears to be evidence to show that even very good readers do regress now and then. Inadequate recognition or a poor vocabulary may cause some regressions. The kind of material read may in some instances also influence regressions. However, there can be no doubt about the bottom line on this controversy—speed readers very seldom regress.

Mark the following statements either True (T), False (F), or Not Mentioned (N) in the space provided.

1. It is agreed that regressions are permissible at times. _____
2. The length of the line of type has an effect on regression. _____
3. Vocabulary and recognition can be factors causing regression. _____
4. There appears to be evidence that good readers do not regress. _____
5. Whether or not you regress may depend on what you are reading. _____

Time/Sec.	7	10	12	15	20	25	30	35	40	45
WPM	1054	738	615	492	369	295	246	210	185	164

If your time isn't shown, divide the number of seconds it took you to read the paragraph into 7380. Be sure to record your progress in the back. (For answers, see page 151.)

Chapter 3

CORRECTING BAD HABITS

There are three major types of readers, and everyone falls into one of these categories. Once you know what type of reader you are, you can improve your technique.

MOTOR READERS

The first type is the *motor reader*. The term *motor* as used here is synonymous with movement. Motor readers move some part of the body as they read. They might wiggle their ears or nose. Maybe they chew gum or twitch an eyebrow as they read along, or maybe they twirl their hair. Perhaps they always tap their fingers or move their Adam's apple as they read. Or they may move their tongue or lips or swing their legs. For them, reading and body movement are synchronized into an intertwined process. Sound silly? It's not. Take away the body movement and you take away these people's reading comprehension, because their reading style is disrupted. For them the faster the reading speed, the faster the body movement.

I was teaching an adult education class in speed reading at a local YMCA. Joe was a college student taking courses because he wanted to go into dentistry and was worried about the amount of required reading he would face in graduate school. During the break on the first night of class, he said to me, "I've never tried to read so fast in all my life." A few minutes later, he said, "For some reason, my legs are killing me." Sure enough, whenever Joe would read, he would shimmy his legs. No wonder he was tired—for him, twenty minutes of fast reading meant twenty minutes of fast leg movements. He was a motor reader. The faster he read, the faster he tried to move his legs.

Then there was Sally, who moved her ears when she read. At slow reading speeds, she moved only her right ear. At higher rates, both ears moved. As a young high-school student with aspirations of becoming a lawyer, she would have a lot of reading to do, and she didn't want to rely on moving her ears to read better and faster.

The problem is that dependency upon moving a part of the body in order to read is a deterrent to fast and efficient reading. It kills reading flexibility and speed, for you can read no faster than you move a part of the anatomy.

Motor readers are the slowest of the three basic types of readers. To correct this habit—and that's what it is, a habit—you first have to become aware of what you're doing. Have somebody watch you read for a few minutes and tell you if you're moving your head or wiggling your nose or twiddling your thumbs while you read. If you are, then you will have to work on eliminating this habit as well as learning the new speed-reading steps as they are presented in this book.

AUDITORY READERS

The second type is the *auditory reader*. Auditory readers usually read faster than motor readers because they don't rely on physical movement. Auditory readers, as the name implies, rely on hearing the words. (The word *auditory* derives from the Latin *audire,* to hear.)

Auditory readers, even in silent reading, form the words as if they were speaking them. At the same time they are seeing the printed symbols, they are hearing the sounds associated with those words. Reliance upon sounding words in order to read means that the reader is slowed down to the rate of oral reading; that is, he can read no faster than he can speak. That's why we also call these readers *vocalizers*.

There are many variations in auditory reading:

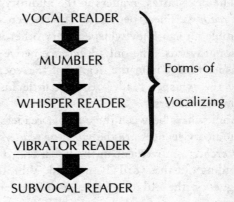

VOCAL READER

MUMBLER

WHISPER READER

VIBRATOR READER

SUBVOCAL READER

Forms of Vocalizing

Let's look at *vocal readers,* who are the slowest in the group of auditory readers. Vocal readers actually say the words aloud as they read. You've probably heard these readers. They think they're reading to themselves, but everyone around them can hear them. Auditory readers usually are unaware of their vocalizing. When it's brought to their attention, it is not uncommon for them to say, "I have to say the words as I read them. If I don't, I can't comprehend anything." This really is not the case, as we shall soon see.

Those on the next level, the *mumblers,* aren't much faster in terms of reading rates, but, since mumbling is quicker than saying each word distinctly, the mumbler reader is a little faster than the vocal reader. Mumblers say the words almost under their breath. Sometimes they sound as though they're humming their way through the printed page. It is not uncommon to see someone use this method when reading intensely. Relying on hearing the words as they are softly mumbled definitely slows reading speed and makes the reading process awkward and cumbersome. What's more, it is not essential for comprehension, which is the reason most mumblers give for continuing to use this "technique."

The next-fastest readers in the auditory group are the *whisper readers*. These people don't say each word aloud or even mumble along. They whisper every other word or perhaps occasional words. The only difference between a mumbler and a whisper reader is in the degree of the vocalization, and that's why the whisper reader reads a little faster than vocal and mumbler readers.

Somewhere between the whisper readers and the next group of auditory readers are the *vibrator readers*. These people usually create a movement in the vocal chords for the purpose of sounding out the words being read. Vibrator readers move the tongue or the Adam's apple as they read. Sometimes such movement cannot even be seen. Try to see if you are a vibrator reader. Place a pencil in your mouth or chew gum while you read. Do you feel your tongue move? Or place your fingers on your Adam's apple and read. Do you feel vibration? If you answer yes to either of these questions, you unconsciously use part of your voice mechanism to sound out words as you read. Your reading is geared to that auditory process, which is holding back your reading speed. Just think how much faster you could read if you weren't waiting for those sound vibrations!

Then there are the *subvocalizers*. This is actually the trickiest form of auditory reading. There is no vocalization of words out loud, no mumbling, no whispering, and no vibrations. The subvocalizer hears each word *mentally* as he or she reads—thus the term *sub* (meaning "under") vocalizer.

The auditory reading process is, in my opinion, largely a result of learning to read by the phonics method of sounding out each word or letter or group of letters. It works like this:

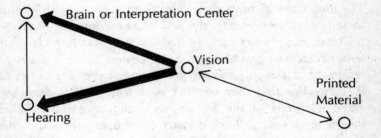

The vision picks up the printed symbols and sends an image of the symbol (letter, word, etc.) to the brain. Simultaneously, that same visual cue triggers a sound (associated with the printed symbol) and also sends that to the brain. Both signals converge in the reader's interpretation center, and this process results in auditory reading. If the auditory signal does not come through loud and clear, comprehension is about zero. Remember, the auditory reader relies on *hearing* the words in order to achieve comprehension. A perfect example is the story about a neighbor of mine. His driver's license had expired, and he had to take the exam to get a new one. He passed the eye test. He passed the driving test. But he flunked the written exam. When I asked him what happened, he said, "I had my new false teeth in, so I couldn't pronounce any of the words on the written test. That's why I didn't understand any of it. If I can't pronounce the words, I can't read anything."

But the strangest aspect about auditory readers is the conditions under which they enjoy reading. They like to read in either of two quite different environments.

Most auditory readers need quiet in order to read, so that they can hear the words mentally and sound them out to themselves as they are reading. It's almost as if they are holding a conversation with themselves. They are reading, but they are also sounding out or saying each word mentally. Noisy conditions interfere with this auditory process in the reader's brain. The loud noise disrupts the reader's conversation with him or herself or, more precisely, the flow of sound into the brain.

Once, many years ago, I taught a speed-reading class for senior citizens at a nearby retirement center. There was a large fan in the classroom, and the group said at the very outset of the first class that they couldn't read with such noise. They asked me to turn off the fan "so they could concentrate." What they wanted was to have it quiet enough to subvocalize the words they were reading. They were auditory readers. You might ask—all of them? Yes, all of them.

Unfortunately, the teaching of reading is sometimes like fashion trends—what's in one year isn't necessarily in the next year. For many years teaching by phonics, or auditory reading, was in. Then teaching by the sight-reading method came back. There is much controversy among reading experts about which method of teaching reading is better: phonics or sight. The pros and cons of this topic have been debated for many years. Neither side has ever gained enough conclusive proof to totally substantiate its case and thereby eliminate the opposition. And so the debate continues and the teaching of reading varies from one generation to another.

Quite often, you can guess how people read just by their age because of the reading style that was taught during the time when they were learning to read. In the case of the senior citizens group, we surveyed the group and found they had indeed all learned to read by phonics. So for that group and this kind of reader in general, quiet conditions are essential or, at the very least, greatly preferred.

Another condition favored by some auditory-phonics readers is to read under the opposite set of circumstances—in other words, noise. It's hard to believe, but some auditory readers prefer to read when there is some noise around! This is especially true for today's young auditory readers, who like to study or read with TV or music as a background. They become so engrossed in hearing themselves mentally as they read along that if someone turns off the TV, the world seems to suddenly come crashing down. The TV or radio is actually a background cover so they can concentrate on the hearing-reading process. This background sound blocks out many of the little extraneous noises that would otherwise interrupt this kind of auditory reader. If it is totally quiet and then a little noise comes from somewhere else in the house, this type of reader loses concentration. Such auditory readers do better when they read in a noisy environment.

When I was going to college I can remember very distinctly seeing these two types of auditory readers. One type could read, and preferred to read, where it was noisy or with a radio or TV on. In such an environment, the students could read and mentally hear the words, with all the hubbub covering any distractions. The other type of auditory reader could be found in the library. I'd walk by and see students reading and forming the sounds of the words with their lips. In both situations the readers relied on hearing words in order to read. Their speed was correlated to hearing and saying the words—aloud or mentally.

SIGHT READERS

The last major type of readers are the *sight readers*. Sight reading is the instant understanding of the printed symbol without auditory association. It is the fastest form of reading because it does not involve reliance on sound or physical movement. Thus, reading speed and comprehension are not hindered by an additional activity. Sight readers see a word or group of words and instantly perceive a visual image along with the meaning associated with the printed symbol. This is why sight readers read so much faster than motor readers and auditory readers. The time required for them to obtain meaning from the printed code is less than it is for the other two types of readers. Sight readers usually have an easier time learning to speed read because they have fewer habits to break and fewer factors slowing down their WPM. Auditory and motor readers just take a little longer to learn to speed read; that is, more time and practice is required.

One thing is sure: Regardless of what kind of reading a person does, he or she cannot rely on physical movements or auditory processes when reading fast. You may have seen demonstrations of speed reading. Well, did you ever see a speed reader waiting until his or her ears moved or vocalizing to hear how the words sounded in order to read faster? On the contrary, a speed reader zips over paragraphs and flies through the pages at a rate that seems fantastic to the novice. Such speed readers use the very same techniques you're now reading about.

Once you know which of the three types of readers you are, how can you improve? For instance, if you're a motor reader, what can you do to increase your reading speed? First, find out which part of the body you're moving. Then you have to stop moving that part of yourself and concentrate on speed. This may not be as easy as it appears because an initial loss in comprehension usually occurs when a motor reader first stops using the motor process. This comprehension loss is soon overcome by time and practice. Then comprehension is even better, for it no longer is dependent on moving a part of your body.

Did you ever see the frustrated look of someone trying to read in a noisy place? It takes a long time to read when you have to re-read the passages because you're grasping for the sounds. As you cut down on vocalizing or relying on auditory reading, your attention shifts from the sounding of words to the meaning of words. You no longer rely on the sound of every word, so you read faster. Push yourself to go faster. Get some speed! If you have to, you'll still hear enough to get the meaning. In the meantime, you're constantly reducing your reliance on the auditory reading process. Go for the WPM! Go faster than you think you should. You've got to get moving. Stretch your abilities.

As with learning any new skill, you can best master speed reading by practice. Try speed reading the next three paragraphs with no regressions, no physical movements, and no auditory processes. Try not to go so fast that you lose all comprehension. It took you a long time to learn to read, and it takes some time and practice to re-learn or master new techniques. Go for some speed using the techniques explained thus far. You'll see how much better you're doing already, compared to how you read before you bought this book and started on this program.

Think of these paragraphs as exercises or calisthenics—you're going to push yourself to do your fastest and best time yet.

Record your time in seconds. Go for speed. Ready? Begin.

Reading #4

RECYCLING ALUMINUM CANS

Recycling aluminum cans conserves energy. In fact, recycling saves 95 percent of the energy needed to make new aluminum from ore. Last year, the aluminum industry saved enough energy through recycling to meet the residential electrical needs of a city the size of Pittsburgh for about six years. Since 1970, aluminum-can recycling has created over 40,000 new jobs at recycling centers. Do your part to help recycle cans and save energy.

Mark the following statements either True (T), False (F) or Not Mentioned (N).

1. Recycling aluminum cans saves energy. _____
2. Since 1970 almost 10,000 jobs have been created at recycling centers. _____
3. By collecting aluminum cans, Texans recently raised $245,000 toward the rebuilding of the Battleship Texas. _____
4. By recycling, enough energy was saved to meet the electrical needs of a city the size of Pittsburgh for six years. _____
5. Recycling is the coming thing. _____

Now let's check your progress. Check your seconds to find your WPM. If your time isn't shown below, divide the number of seconds it took you to read the paragraph into 4440. This will give you your exact WPM. For answers to the comprehension quiz, check page 151.

Time/Sec.	3	5	10	12	15	20	25
WPM	1480	888	444	370	296	222	178

Let's try your speed on another paragraph. Time yourself in seconds. Try to accelerate your rate and push for speed. Ready? Begin.

Reading #5

NEW AEROBIC TRAINER

Take the boredom out of your life and get the most out of your workout with a state-of-the-art, new aerobic stationary bicycle exerciser or trainer. You can recreate all the hills and valleys of a cross-country bike tour and be kept fully informed of your progress via a light-emitting-diode control panel. This innovative computerized program provides the same kind of rhythmic interval training used by world-class athletes. Your own pedaling powers an on-board computer that offers numerous programmed ride sequences. It's self-powered and requires no electricity. It'll help you build a better body, increase your physical fitness, and stay in shape.

Mark the following statements either True (T), False (F) or Not Mentioned (N).

1. New aerobic trainers can help you get into shape. _____
2. Aerobic trainers can be self-powered. _____
3. Aerobic trainers came to us from the space training program for the nation's astronauts. _____
4. The trainers require assembly. _____
5. This type of new trainer is boring. _____

Time/Sec.	5	7	10	12	15	17	20	25	30
WPM	1356	968	678	565	452	399	339	271	226

If your time isn't shown, divide the number of seconds it took you to read the paragraph into 6780. Now check your answers for comprehension on page 151. Record the results on your Progress Chart.

Try another exercise. Push for speed.

Reading #6

GONE WITH THE WIND—A UNIQUE MOVIE

It seems unlikely the production of any future movie will ever provide the great impact *Gone with the Wind* did in 1939. The world then was a different place, observed through a different set of values. World War II, VCRs, the Middle East, television—many of our future distractions were yet to come. By all reports, production of *Gone with the Wind* caused a frenzy of excitement, and why not? Press leaks were said to have been sensational. Every big star in Hollywood was after parts; a fistful of famous directors hired and fired; a two-year search for an unknown Scarlett—all this following the unparalleled success of Margaret Mitchell's book *Gone with the Wind,* which tugged the heartstrings of even the most stalwart Northerners. The next time you're at the video center, look for *Gone with the Wind,* and enjoy a major movie event of another generation.

Mark the following questions either True (T), False (F), or Not Mentioned (N).

1. *Gone with the Wind* was a famous movie. _____
2. It was ranked among the all-time top five in gross box-office receipts. _____
3. The movie was made in 1939. _____
4. It took six months to find an actress for the heroine, Scarlett.
_____

5. The movie was based on a book written by Margaret Mitchell.

_____

Time/Sec.	7	10	12	15	17	20	25	30
WPM	1346	942	785	628	554	471	377	314

If your time isn't shown, divide the number of seconds it took you to read this paragraph into 9420. This will give you your exact speed, or WPM. Now check your comprehension by looking up the answers to the quiz on page 151.

Now check your progress. You should have completed readings 1 through 6. You should see a faster reading rate for paragraph #6 compared to the first paragraph you read when you started. Just think what you can do with practice—and after completing this book. You're on your way to better and faster reading. You are in the process of breaking lifelong habits and establishing new ones. Sometimes that takes a while. Sometimes, however, success is instant. It all depends on the individual reader.

Breaking the speed barrier can be fun. Keep at it and see how you can continue developing your newfound reading abilities.

Chapter 4

EYE SPAN AND THOUGHT UNITS

You're now ready for two more key concepts: eye span and thought units. *Eye span*—the fundamental eye movement made by every reader—means how many words the reader sees or reads at one time, in a single glance. *Thought units* are groupings of words according to content, rather than the number of words.

Many people think that the eyes move in continuous motion over each line of print. They don't. They move in jumps and hops in a series of segments over each line. Think of reading as a process like a movie film, which is actually a series of single frames, or pictures, shown at a high rate of speed so that the viewer sees the pictures in a continuous motion. Reading is a similar process: The viewing of a series of words or letters so rapidly that we think our eyes are in continuous motion.

The secret to reading faster then becomes: *The more words you see at one time the faster you read.* Still doubt it? Try this. Ask a friend to read while you watch his or her eyes move. See if they are in continuous motion or if you observe the eyes moving in jumps and jerks as they cover each line of print. If your friend is a slow reader, it will be harder to see the jumps because the eye span is small, whereas a fast reader really clips off the words, so that you can easily see the large, sweeping eye movements.

EYE SPAN

For many people the basis of fantastic improvement in their reading speed and comprehension is simply this—a good eye span. Obviously, if you read one word at a time and then increase this eye span to two or three words at a time, your reading speed will be improved two or three hundred percent! This increase can be extended to four or five words or more—wherever your motivation and energies take you.

Comprehension is also improved by this same process because words and their meanings always have more significance when they are read in association with other words. It's like a puzzle. One small piece doesn't give much suggestion of a picture. Several connected pieces give a much better indication of what the completed puzzle will look like. So it is with reading: The wider the eye span, the faster the reading speed and the bigger the comprehension picture.

With this understanding of one of the most basic eye movements made in reading, many people have embarked on various methods to improve their eye span, or recognition rate. There are various methods and practice techniques that can be utilized to develop a good eye span. You should keep in mind that everyone has a basic rhythm of eye-span movements. These differ or vary from reader to reader. Eye span is one of the key factors in accounting for the difference in people's reading speeds. As you will see in the following examples, there is a significant difference between the eye span of the word-by-word reader and that of the "super-tough" speed reader.

Note that the word-by-word reader reads only one word at a time, while the speed reader sees almost a whole line—or at least half a line—at a time. Each reader in these examples reads from one mark (/) to the next. Read these examples and move your eyes from one mark (/) to the next and you will be able to see the difference eye span makes in reading rates:

WORD-BY-WORD READER

There/is/no/telling/how/many/different/local/times/there/were/in/ the/United/States/prior/to/the/adoption/of/Standard/Time./

A LITTLE FASTER READER

Reports that/a monstrous/white shark/25 to/30 feet/long/ is ranging/ off Montauk,/New York,/on the eastern tip/of Long Island/have divided people/into two camps:/those who/believe the stories/ and those/who don't./

FASTER YET

San Diego is/the oldest city/in California./It is situated/on San Diego Bay./The city is/110 miles/southeast of Los Angeles/and only 15 miles/from the Mexican border./It owes/its importance/to its superb harbor./

SPEED READER

Just exactly what is a bird?/Perhaps you could say/a bird is an animal that flies./But butterflies fly and they are insects,/and bats, which are mammals, also fly./Birds, however, have feathers./No other animal has feathers./Feathers then, and not flying,/make a bird different from other animals./

Note that the faster the reader is, the more words he or she sees at one time. The eye span is greater as the reader reads faster. To become a faster reader you need to train yourself to see at least two to three or four words in a single eye span. This is why many people refer to this eye-span movement as *phrase reading.* In speed reading, you are really reading in phrases, or large groups of words. You learn to do this by increasing your eye span from one word to two words to four words to five words to a whole line at one time.

You read faster and comprehend more by using the eye-span method. Both your speed and comprehension improve as the eye span becomes wider. This method allows you to improve your reading skills while not having to omit or skip any words. This fact offsets the worry many people have about losing comprehension. They want to learn to speed read, but at the same time they don't want to skip any words because they're afraid of missing something. The eye-span method is their answer. Comprehension doesn't suffer; speed improves; and there is no risk of missing any key words that may be critical to understanding or comprehension.

Now try the following eye-span stretching exercises. The object is to train your eyes to use the eye-span method to understand larger groups of words at a single glance and to develop *rhythmic* eye movements that enable you to read quickly and comfortably. This exercise is simply a series of left-to-right eye movements with your eyes reading each phrase. Push yourself and read these as fast as you can while still understanding what you are reading. It won't work unless you go faster than normal. You have to push your reading rate. Hurry!

The national sport
of the United States
is baseball.
For more
than a century,
young and old alike
have enjoyed playing
or watching the game.
  From early spring
until late fall,

players and fans
thrill to the
umpire's heady cry of
"Play ball!"
  From the
rude sandlots to
well-maintained
big league diamonds,
baseball is played
in all the states.
  Every year, more than
36 million spectators
attend games
played by
professional teams.
In addition,
more than
50 million
watch games
played by
organized teams of
semiprofessionals and amateurs.
Radio and TV
carry play-by-play
accounts of games.
Newspapers report
results and records
in great detail.
  In and out
of season
baseball fans
everywhere
discuss the
relative merits
of teams and players.

How was that? Easy! Right? See how reading in groups of even two or three words can really improve your speed and comprehension!

Apply these techniques to the following two paragraphs, using the same procedure. Note your time and comprehension on the Progress Chart so that you can watch your improvement continue to increase. Time yourself in seconds to see how long it takes to read each paragraph. Remember: Avoid regressions, physical movements, and auditory processes, and make more extended eye-span movements.

Reading #7

EYE-SPAN READING

There are probably as many ways of speed reading as there are ways of getting dressed in the morning. However, even in getting dressed, it is necessary to put on certain things first. For example, it is impractical to put on your socks after your shoes. Along the same vein, in speed reading some basic steps must be done first. You must learn to see one or two words at a time before you can accurately see four or five. It is a case of learning to see shorter word groups before trying longer ones. Likewise, phrases are used before attempting sentences. Eye span is one of the keys to speed reading.

Mark the following statements either True (T), False (F), or Not Mentioned (N).

1. There are only one or two ways to speed read. _____
2. Some basic, specific steps must be followed. _____
3. Long words and sentences may be successfully read by the reader at the very beginning. _____

4. To avoid fatigue, reading should be done in a very specific manner. _____

5. Read at one glance from the very beginning. _____

Time/Sec.	5	7	10	12	15	17	20	25
WPM	1416	1011	708	590	472	416	354	283

If your time isn't given above, divide your time, in seconds, into 7080 for your exact WPM. (For answers, see page 151.)

Record your scores on the Progress Chart on page 149, and try the next paragraph.

Reading #8

DARE TO LOVE

She sighed . . . and then felt her heart leap as the double doors suddenly swept open again. Their dark panels framed one of the tallest men she had ever seen, lithe and erect, wearing knee boots of gleaming leather moulded to the strong calves of his legs. Blue denims were belted into a flat, athletic waist, and a fine white T-shirt covered a broad chest and a pair of wide shoulders. The neck of his T-shirt was open against a suntanned throat, and as her gaze rose to his face . . . she knew instantly why she had been fascinated by and dared to love this man. Stories like this are more fun to read if you can speed read!

Mark the following statements either True (T), False (F), or Not Mentioned (N).

1. He wore tan breeches. _____
2. She was a tall, statuesque blonde. _____

3. He was one of the tallest men she had ever seen.
   _____

4. She knew instantly why she dared to love him. _____
5. He had on an open blazer. _____

Time/Sec.	5	7	10	12	17	20	25
WPM	1488	1063	744	620	438	372	298

If your time isn't shown, divide your time, in seconds, into 7440 for your WPM.

Apply this eye-span technique periodically to your everyday reading. Many magazines (for example, *Reader's Digest* and *Sports Illustrated*) are very good for practicing these speed-reading methods. In fact, most magazines are good for this purpose because they have only five to eight words per line, and narrow columns are more conducive to the eye-span type of reading. Researchers have found that this is a major reason why magazines are so popular. Not only do they contain interesting topics, they are also very easy to read because of the narrow-column format. Magazines have two, three, or four narrow columns per page, while most books have just one column across the entire page.

Books, such as some histories that have very wide columns, are especially difficult to read because they require such a wide eye-span movement to get across the page. The same reasoning applies to newspapers: The front page is easier to read because the columns are narrow; the editorial section is harder because the columns are generally much wider. The vocabulary level of the two pages isn't actually much different, despite myths to the contrary. Magazines and paperback books with small columns and a significant amount of white space (the area between lines and words) are easy to read and conducive to practicing speed reading.

THOUGHT UNITS

The thought-unit approach is very much like the eye-span method, but with a unique twist. The idea here is to acquire the habit of *reading one thought after another, regardless of the number of words involved*. This requires a lot of flexibility on the part of the reader because he or she has to vary eye movements in order to accommodate the various lengths of the thoughts. This technique stresses that all concentration should be devoted to grasping the author's thoughts and ideas. The expansion of the eye span from one word to two words, and so on, is underplayed in favor of concentrating on the large blocks of thoughts presented in the writing.

For instance, here is how a paragraph may be read by the thought-unit approach:

Today is March 22nd./It is a beautiful day./It is also my birthday./ I wonder/who'll remember that?/

Proponents of the thought-unit theory say you shouldn't take in just any group of words—you should take in groups of ideas. The exact unit of thought is subject to the reader's interpretation of what constitutes that basic thought.

The only drawback to the thought-unit method is that it often requires more flexibility than the average reader possesses. Most readers begin by reading one word at a time in horizontal sequence across each line. To expect them to shift to a varying eye pattern that is never the same is a lot to ask. However, it is an excellent technique if you can master it because it offers a greater potential for speed, or WPM.

Regardless of whether you like the eye-span method or the thought-unit approach, reading experts agree that one of the basic secrets of speed reading is taking in large, meaningful groups of words at one glance. The person who looks at each word or perhaps at only two words at a glance is able to pick up only small scraps of ideas. Such a practice retards his speed and impairs his comprehension. Therefore it is important to cultivate the habit of taking in as large an "eyeful" of words as you can at each glance.

Practice forcing yourself to read as fast as you can. If you consciously strive to read faster for a while, new speed patterns will replace the old ones, and rapid reading will become a permanent habit. The following paragraph shows you how to grasp meaningful word groups or thought units. See if you can take in an entire group of words at each glance. Push your mental tempo as fast as you possibly can, while still getting the idea expressed in each word group.

RUNNING THE FOOTBALL

In professional football circles/coaches like Woody Hayes and George Allen/were known for their safe approach/to the game. By sticking mainly with running plays,/they avoided costly turn-overs/that haunted coaches/who shot for huge gains/by passing repeatedly.

Of course/being conservative by itself/doesn't guarantee victory./You still have to gain/at least ten yards every four plays/to move the ball/down the field. By emphasizing good blocking,/mistake-free execution, and solid fundamentals,/these coaches consistently achieved decent yardage/from running plays—not to mention/a truckload of victories.

Divide the selection that follows into thought groups as you see them. There's no right or wrong way. Just make a short mark between the word groups as was done in the preceding paragraph. After you have divided the paragraph into thought units, see if you can re-read the paragraph quickly, taking in each thought unit with one swift eye glance. This new skill takes time and practice to learn, but applying it to everyday reading will soon pay off for you!

THE EARTH

Our blue planet. Our green planet. It was worth the 21 billion dollars spent on the Apollo space mission to make us perceive, through the eyes of the astronauts and with our own eyes, the color and inviting richness of the earth in contrast to the bleakness of outer space. Now that we have experienced the grayness and drabness of the moon and now that the photographs taken by the Mariner spacecrafts have dispelled our illusions about the existence of canals and life on Mars, we appreciate even more the sensuous appeal of Earth with her blue atmosphere and green mantle. Our planet is responsible, in part, for our very nature because human beings are shaped biologically and mentally by the environment in which they develop. We should all do our part to preserve the quality of our earth and our co-existence with it.

Basically, these two approaches—eye-span and thought-unit—are saying the same thing to the person who is learning to speed read. That is, *increased reading speed and comprehension are dependent upon reading larger and larger word groups.* The technique you use is really up to you. It is important to try both methods and then to stick with the one that gives you the best results and feels most comfortable.

Everyone can learn to read in larger eye spans or thought units with a reasonable amount of practice. You just have to keep at it until you have it mastered. Your reward will be a reading speed that is much faster than you ever thought possible, and you'll find that your comprehension has also improved.

But don't be overly concerned about your comprehension at

this early stage of the game. Concentrate on each step as it is presented. Study all the new techniques until you've mastered them. Then you can concentrate on the content. First you eliminate regressions, then you avoid physical movements and auditory habits, then you increase your eye span. Comprehension will follow. It may surprise you, but there's a lot of similarity in learning to type and learning to speed read. They both involve eye movements. A good typing teacher will tell you that at first you have to sacrifice accuracy and start to practice typing faster. Once your typing speed is where you want it, then you work at accuracy. So it is in reading with speed and comprehension; but we'll delve into this in more detail in chapter 8. Right now just concentrate on following these techniques as they are presented and getting your reading speed going.

Before we leave this chapter, let us address ourselves to one last argument occasionally heard in the field of speed reading. This is the theory that reading is not primarily a physical act involving eye movements, but a psychological process that takes place in the reader's mind. That argument, followed to its logical conclusion, would mean that in order to improve a reader we should send him or her to a psychologist. Or does it mean that to teach speed reading we should deal with the way a person thinks instead of how he or she actually reads? To me, this is like saying that people who want to lose weight should think about their mental processes instead of watching their diet and counting calories. It is usually through becoming aware of what we are eating, re-educating ourselves as to the caloric value of different foods, and consuming fewer calories that we lose weight. So it is with reading. First you become aware of your eye patterns; then you learn to speed read by eliminating unnecessary eye movements and replacing them with more efficient ones. Isn't that what a doctor tells a patient on a diet to do—replace certain foods with more efficient ones? Obesity and slow reading are the results of excessive movements; one is toward food in the refrigerator that is not needed; the other is toward eye movements that aren't needed.

In any event, it is easier to teach a person how to count calories and how to speed read than to deal with the psychology of mind processes.

As you read from now on, remember: No regressions. No vocalizing. No subvocalizing. No motor reading. Move right along. Push forward every time you feel the urge to regress. Don't linger on any words. Just keep moving! Don't worry about your comprehension right now. It will come along. Stretch your eye span. Keep on reading and using these techniques. Use them every day. You're on your way to better and faster reading!

Chapter 5

MORE TECHNIQUES THAT WORK

RETURN EYE SWEEP

Another eye movement that is critical to a good reading speed is called *return eye sweep*. This is the movement that your eyes make as they go from the end of one line to the beginning of the next. It should be a very rapid movement, just as the word "sweep" implies. The eyes should have a return motion that is smooth, rapid, and rhythmic.

The drill on this and the next page is designed to make you conscious of the correct eye movements to be made during the return sweeps. Read the paragraph quickly. Your eyes should make two eye spans or jumps per each line of the paragraph. At the end of the line, make your eyes follow the dotted arrows that show you the return-eye-sweep pattern.

Sweep your eyes   down and back

←←←←←←←←

to the next line.   Never stop

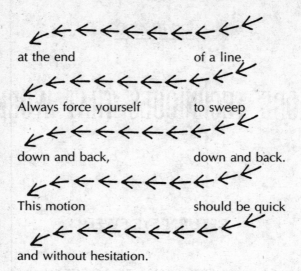

at the end   of a line.

Always force yourself   to sweep

down and back,   down and back.

This motion   should be quick

and without hesitation.

Did you feel the sweep of your eyes? Now go back and try to read this same exercise even more rapidly. Race your eyes along the arrows. Never give your eyes a chance to stop or waver as they move from the end of one line to the beginning of the next. This forcefulness and direct movement is the key to improving your return sweep. If your eyes waver, they may lose the place. If your eyes linger or hesitate, your reading speed suffers. If your eyes move quickly and smoothly on the return sweep, they will reach their destination accurately, and your reading rate will be much faster.

Read this next paragraph just as you read the paragraph in the preceding exercise. There are no return arrows in this second example, but you should still make your eyes follow the same swift pattern that is necessary for good return eye sweep:

Pause to read.   But never pause
on the return sweep.   Move quickly, smoothly.
A reader must practice   a smooth return sweep.

A reader must practice	eliminating regressions.
A reader must practice	wide recognition spans.
Did your eyes reach	their destination
on every line?	

Practice your return sweep. Use the narrow columns on the front page of any newspaper or magazine. As you read, make yourself conscious of a smooth, fast return motion; sweep back and down to the next line. Time is critical. This movement must be rapid with no wasted effort. The correct rapid-return eye-sweep process can easily help to speed up your reading and improve your comprehension as well. One reader I had in a university class would spend time daydreaming on each return eye sweep. Her return sweeps were so slow that she once said to me, "I almost forgot what I've read by the time I get to the next line." For her, the return-eye-sweep technique helped the most in improving her reading speed.

Now try the following two paragraphs and see if you can speed up your return-eye-sweep.

Reading #9

EARLY CHILD CARE

If Pulitzer prizes were awarded for attracting public interest, surely the issue of early child care would be a strong contender this year. Hardly a day passes without major national and local coverage by broadcast and print media. Most of the media attention focuses on the benefits of early childhood education as a means to reduce work-related family stress as well as to increase the social and academic competence of the youngsters. Availability and quality of services and programs are being discussed in every statehouse in the land, in the White House, and on Capitol Hill. Interest in educating young children is at an all-time high. Even corporations have launched such services for their employees, their children, and their families. The concept of early child care is finally coming into its own.

Mark the following statements either True (T), False (F), or Not Mentioned (N).

1. Interest in early child care is at an all-time high. _____
2. Most of the media attention focuses on the benefits of early childhood education. _____
3. The child-care centers in the eastern states are more progressive. _____
4. Some corporations even offer day-care services for their employees. _____
5. There is significant governmental interest in child-care centers._____

Time/Sec.	5	7	10	12	15	17	20	25
WPM	1768	1263	884	736	589	520	442	353

If your time isn't shown, divide your time, in seconds, into 8840 for your WPM.

Reading #10

THE NEED FOR BETTER READING SKILLS

The mysteries of higher mathematics with all its complex formulas and theorems cannot be mastered or even approached until one has mastered basic addition, subtraction, multiplication, and division. In fact, most people would want more familiarity with the fundamentals of math than just how to add and subtract and would try maybe algebra or geometry before tackling calculus. However, we frequently find people trying to read from the printed page before they have mastered the basic fundamentals in the reading process. The easy and effective use of a complex skill such as speed reading or higher math comes only after a mastery of the knowledge of the fundamentals upon which the skill is based.

Mark the following statements either True (T), False (F), or Not Mentioned (N).

1. Simple arithmetic should precede complex theorems. _____

2. Effective speed reading can be mastered by anyone. _____

3. Speed reading has certain fundamentals just like math. _____

4. Reading is seldom attempted without adequate preparation. _____

5. Fundamentals aren't really essential in skill mastery. _____

Time/Sec.	5	7	10	12	15	20	25	30
WPM	1452	1037	726	605	484	363	290	242

If your time isn't shown, divide your time, in seconds, into 7260 for your exact WPM. Be sure you're recording all your comprehension and WPM scores in the appropriate spaces on the Progress Chart on page 149. (For answers, see page 151.)

FIXATIONS

The next eye movement is called a *fixation*. Fixations are the stops or pauses between eye spans. When you read, your eyes move in jumps. They fix upon a part of a line, make a hop, pause for an instant, hop again, and then the whole process is repeated. This process occurs line after line and page after page. Watch another person's eyes while he is reading. You will see him chew up a line of type in separate bites, like someone eating corn on the cob. This describes the basic reading procedure followed by most people. It is a series of movements and stops.

The stop, or pause, during which the eyes are momentarily at rest, is the fixation. Scientists tell us that during the reading process this is the only time that vision is registered. In the quick motion between pauses, the eyes do not register vision. To the reader, however, the eyes seem to be in continuous motion.

EYE SPAN   FIXATIONS

Reading would be a slow, awkward process if the eyes did not see and register like lightning so that everything seems to be in continuous motion. In reading, the eyes function like a motion-picture camera. The eyes capture a series of printed symbols with such rapidity that these symbols are blended into what seems to be a series of continuous visual impressions that convey the author's thoughts to the reader.

Slow-motion pictures are fun to watch every once in a while; they are unusual and so slow, so unnatural, that we react by laughing because we know they are exaggerated or unreal. However, viewing slow-motion pictures for any length of time soon becomes boring. Our mind starts to wander. We begin to think of other things. So it is in the reading process. We have to read at a good rate without long stops or fixations or our mind will begin to daydream or wander from what we are reading. Sometimes we refer to this lapse as a lack of concentration when, actually, lengthy fixations are to blame.

The eyes can change their fixation performance in two ways: They can *reduce the length of time for each fixation* and they can *reduce the number of fixations*. For example, your eyes right now hop along this line in a pattern that you can consciously direct. You can make your eyes distinguish each letter or word, if you wish. You can make your eyes fix on one letter or one word. The number of stops your eyes make and how long your eyes are stopped are the two keys in the fixation procedure. Think of a pit stop in auto racing. Periodically, every car has to make one. The number of stops and the length of each stop have a lot to do with a racer's overall speed and whether or not he wins. This is also true in speed reading. Too many or too long pit stops, or fixations, will mean that you lose the race for speed, or WPM.

Working with the fixation pauses in the following sentences will give you practice in examining your stop-and-go eye movements. Read these phrases very quickly and *focus on each dot as briefly as you can*. When you have finished the paragraph, take the quiz that follows.

•   •   •
As you read   try to push   your eyes ahead.
        •   •
Your eyes   stop-and-go,   stop-and-go
        •   •   •
across the line.   Each "go" movement   is very fast;
        •   •   •
it is merely   a quick dart.   Your eyes read
        •   •
one each stop.   Make each stop   as short
        •   •
as possible.   Do not linger   on any word.

Choose the word that completes each statement correctly.

1. You should not linger on any (a) idea, (b) sentence, (c) word.
2. Each "go" movement is a (a) pause, (b) dart, (c) stop.

Here are some examples that are actual replications of the

basic eye movements made by three adults as each one read the
same line of print. The vertical lines represent the points at
which their eyes rested or fixed as they moved across the line.
The numbers at the top of the vertical lines represent the order
in which the fixations took place. The numbers at the bottom
of the vertical lines represent the length of time for each fixation (measured in sixteenths of a second).

```
    1           2             3
The time is now for all good men to come to the . . .
    9           7             5

    1       2       3       5   4   6           7
The time is now for all good men to come to the . . .
    6       9       6       6   8   7           9

  1   2   4   3   5   7     6       8   10  9
The time is now for all good men to come to the . . .
 30   2  18   5   6   4    10      12   26  4
```

Notice the sequence of fixations for the first reader. It was
1–2–3 right in a row. But look at the second reader who went
1–2–3–5–4. This sequence shows a regression. Now look at
the third reader. Notice how long the first fixation took in
comparison to the second. That isn't uncommon, because the
first fixation in a line often takes longer. Note the length of the
fourth fixation compared to the third. This isn't uncommon
because fixations made during regressions are almost always
longer than those made as you read along going forward. Think
how much faster this third reader would be if he did two things
about his fixations: (1) reduced the number of fixations he made
and (2) reduced how long his eyes fixed at one time. His reading speed would immediately be much faster; his comprehension would also be improved since his thought processes would
be more rapid and continuous.

Fragmented reading due to long fixations is like listening to
someone who stutters; comprehension is difficult and slow.

There is no doubt that correcting these two fixation habits can help speed up the reading process. In rapid reading it is important that the reader's fixations be of short duration and that the number of fixations not be excessive. *If you cultivate the habit of rapidly picking up one thought after another and do not make the common mistake of stopping or fixing upon each punctuation mark, your reading speed will be much faster.*

As an elementary-school principal, I remember observing a primary teacher who said to the children: "A period means stop. You should come to a complete halt and rest the eyes on that punctuation mark we call a period. Count to yourself 1–2–3 every time you see a period and then you can go on to the next sentence."

Well, I have news for that teacher; a period doesn't mean stop. A period is just a little tool or symbol we use to separate one thought from another. A sentence is usually defined as a complete thought; so as long as young readers don't have difficulty running the thoughts or sentences together, the teacher should not slow down their reading speed by teaching them to fixate for long periods of time and thus make reading a tiring and cumbersome task. Reading can be fun and rapid. Those fixations that you do make should be brief and fast-moving. Both speed and comprehension are improved by mastering this one step.

Apply this newest technique to the following paragraph. Make as few fixations as possible. Make your eyes zip right along. When you feel them stop momentarily, get them going again and keep them going. Be sure to time yourself, and use the standard procedure we've been using to track your progress.

Reading #11

PEDIATRICIANS AND WORKING MOTHERS

Are today's pediatricians different? You bet they are. Pediatricians have forged a new healthy medical alliance with today's working mothers. Many pediatricians have expanded their practices to accommodate working mothers: 50 percent now offer regular weekend hours, and 48 percent now offer regular evening hours. About 97 percent of the pediatricians provide 24-hour emergency phone numbers. Only 37 percent welcome calls from the child care provider, but the number is on the increase. Almost 59 percent of today's pediatricians have regular phone hours for non-urgent questions. About 62 percent of today's working mothers say they are content with their pediatricians, and another 35 percent are satisfied. And last but not least is that 95 percent of the working mothers say their doctors do not make them feel guilty about working. In this era of dual incomes and dual careers, such statistics are all good news.

Mark the following either True (T), False (F), or Not Mentioned (N):

1. Today's pediatricians are different. _____
2. Few pediatricians offer regular weekend hours. _____
3. The American Academy of Pediatrics says most pediatricians are married and have at least one child under eighteen. _____
4. Today's working mothers are satisfied with their pediatricians. _____
5. Women pediatricians are more sympathetic to working mothers than men are. _____

Time/Sec.	2	3	5	7	10	12	15	20
WPM	4500	3000	1800	1285	900	750	600	450

If your time isn't shown, divide your time, in seconds, into 9000 for your exact WPM. Be sure to chart your progress on page 149.

The paragraph you have just read is different from all the preceding ones in this book in one major aspect, which is why it was placed here: It has a lot of numbers in it. Perhaps you hadn't noticed that all the previous paragraphs and readings contained very few numbers. The reason for this is quite simple: Reading numbers requires the reader to make more fixations than reading words does. This is why whenever we are reading along and suddenly encounter a date or number, we make a long fixation at that point. We kind of burn the number into our memory, as part of the fixation process. Whenever you see numbers, be aware of the fixations you make and how they affect your reading rate.

If you want to read numbers faster, the secret is the same as reading words—put them into groups. In other words, to read words faster you read more than one word at a time. The same is true in order to read numbers faster—read them in groups of two or three. This process will easily triple your reading speed on numbers and increase your accuracy at the same time.

CONFIGURATION

To understand why we fixate more on numbers than on words, we have to understand *configuration*. In the world of reading, configuration refers to the distinct size and shape of a word. Take the word "good." It has a distinct size and shape (or configuration).

There are very few other words that have the very same configuration. In essence, as we grow older and gain experience in reading and have seen the same word many times, we cease to read the word closely and instead recognize it by its configuration. Try to figure out the following sentence by configuration. I'll give you a few helpful hints by placing some letters throughout the sentence to aid you in deciphering it.

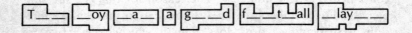

Figure it out? If you did, you read it by configuration. The sentence says: "The boy was a good football player."

We all do this everyday. If you've been driving for a long time, you don't "read" the stop signs in the same manner you did when you first learned to drive. You read them by configuration. You see the shape of the sign and know what it says.

It might surprise you to learn that numbers, unlike words, have very little configuration. It's because of this that numbers are harder to read and require more fixations. In fact, that's what prompted an old friend of mine to call on me for some advice. Dick is a CPA. He said it wasn't unusual for him to take several hours to read the newspaper in the evening. He wanted to take a speed-reading course and asked where he could find such a class offered.

Dick's reading style grew out of his habit of fixing on numbers every day in his work. For an accountant, accuracy is critical. However, he carried over his fixation reading habit into his leisure, or pleasure, reading. Many people who deal with figures every day—bankers, accountants, stockbrokers, and insurance agents—tend to incorporate lengthy fixations into their reading style.

Try to read the following series of numbers and you'll see how many more fixations it takes to read numbers. Read each line across in a horizontal manner, left to right:

NUMBER EXERCISE

2

4 5

6 8 7

4 2 1 5

9 3 2 1 7

1 0 6 3 3 4

2 1 6 9 5 7 3

5 6 5 7 1 5 4 3

6 7 8 2 3 1 9 9 0

4

3 2

9 8 4

4 2 3 7

9 4 3 1 0

5 4 0 9 8 7

6 9 2 4 3 2 1

7 4 3 2 5 6 8 8

8 2 3 7 6 1 0 9 3

If you were aware of your eye movements as you read those numbers, you would have noticed that after you reached four numbers in a row, you were making fixations on at least two or three numbers per line. You must have also noticed that you couldn't read numbers by configuration. Look at the next-to-last set of numbers. It has no distinct configuration compared to a word. The word "educated" has eight letters instead of eight digits as in the next-to-last set of numbers. Yet it is much easier to read and remember "educated" than 74325688.

Now try the following paragraph, which contains no numbers. *Go for speed.* You will notice how much easier it is to read because there are no numbers.

Reading #12

EXERCISE

Anything from a gym workout to a brisk walk benefits beyond physical fitness. It's good for mental health, too. Exercise reduces stress and tension and helps you sleep better. It improves concentration. It can even lift your spirits. Make regular exercise a part of your life.

Mark the following statements either True (T), False (F), or Not Mentioned (N).

1. Exercise helps reduce stress. _____
2. Exercise has no effect on sleep. _____
3. Most adults exercise thirty minutes daily. _____
4. Exercise improves concentration. _____
5. We should all make regular exercise a part of our lives. _____

Time/Sec.	2	3	4	5	6	8	10
WPM	1440	960	720	576	480	360	288

If your time isn't shown, divide your time, in seconds, into 2880 for your WPM. Write your WPM and comprehension scores on your Progress Chart.

Chapter 6

MEASURING AND PRACTICING YOUR NEW READING SKILLS

It's important to know how and what to practice if you are going to continue mastering the art of speed reading. Your reading ability can be improved if you: (1) want to improve, (2) know how to improve, and (3) practice. By working with this book, you've already demonstrated a desire to improve, so step one has already been accomplished. Knowing how to improve depends to a great extent on my success as author in showing you the methods or techniques for improving your reading. Since you're now up to chapter 6, we're making progress on this second step. This brings us to step three: *practice*. This last one is really up to you, and that's what this chapter is all about. Research has shown that with practice the average person can make at least a 20 percent improvement in reading rate.

There is no one established pattern for practice that is applicable to everyone. That's the beauty of the methods found in this book—flexibility. For instance, you can choose the old, proven, standby procedure of setting aside a time for practice each day. That's been a time-tested and successful way of learning almost anything. Or you could do the opposite—have no established time for practice and just incorporate the techniques found in this book into your daily reading whenever you can. This is a gradual, periodic process.

We'll explore these two different methods in more detail in just a bit, but first let's see how to measure your reading speed on material you read from a magazine, journal, nonfiction book, or your favorite novel. Then we can incorporate this procedure into our explanation of practicing by the two different methods.

MEASURING YOUR READING SPEED

First you have to remember where you begin to read. Maybe place a mark (✔) where you start. Then read as fast as you can but still read with understanding. You are aiming for speed—not sheer recklessness at all costs. Reading so fast that you cannot follow the author's thoughts will accomplish nothing. Yet you have to keep in mind, too, that you still have to work at cranking up your reading speed. The whole idea of this book is to learn to speed read, and you'll learn that best by doing it. So at this stage, your primary objective is speed! When you finish reading your selection, make another mark (✔) where you finish.

In addition to keeping track of where you started and finished, you will want to ascertain—in seconds—how long it took you to read the material. The length of the reading is up to you, but, at the outset of learning to speed read, shorter readings of one to four paragraphs will be better for your purposes.

Next you must find the total number of words in what you have read. This is called the *word count*. An easy way to do this is to count the number of words in one line of average length, then multiply that by the number of lines you have read. This way you don't have to count each word. When counting words, remember that contractions, hyphenated words, or numbers with decimal points or commas are counted as two words.

The third step is to multiply the word count by 60. This gives us a result that we call *total words*. Then divide the total words by the number of seconds it took you to read that material. Now you have your exact reading speed in words per minute (WPM). The whole process of finding your reading rate goes like this:

Finishing time: _____
Starting time: =_____
Reading time: _____(seconds)

$$\frac{\rule{3cm}{0.4pt}}{\text{Word Count}} \times 60 = \frac{\rule{3cm}{0.4pt}}{\text{Total words}}$$

$$\frac{\rule{3cm}{0.4pt}}{\text{Total words}} \div \frac{\rule{2cm}{0.4pt}}{\text{seconds}} = \frac{\rule{2cm}{0.4pt}}{\text{WPM}}$$

Here's a sample calculation:

Finishing time: 1:30:51 P.M.
Starting time: 1:30:30 P.M.
Reading time: 21 (seconds)

Word count 118 × 60 = Total words 7080
Total words 7080 ÷ 21 seconds = 337 WPM

This procedure is a simple method to convert time in seconds to words per minute. You can use it daily to check on your reading speed for whatever material you choose to read. You simply need two pieces of information:

1. The number of words in the selection you have read.
2. The number of seconds it took you to read it.

Another way to look at this process is:

$$\frac{\text{number of words in selection} \times 60 = \text{(total words)}}{\text{time in seconds}} = \text{WPM}$$

Timed practice with light, easy-to-read nonfictional material is best. Technical material is difficult to use as a basis for practice when you are learning this new skill. Concentrate first on speed; comprehension and recall will follow. Probably the hardest aspect of speed reading is worrying about comprehension. Learning to read faster is like learning to swim faster or to run faster. At first, things seem awkward. It takes time and practice before the new ways feel comfortable, easy, and natural. If you want to test your comprehension on these timed practice readings, see if you can jot down or recall the author's main points. Try to remember the basic plot or major points of the story. Then hand the article, book, or magazine to a friend or family member and ask him or her to quiz you about what you have just read.

Here's a sample reading for your application of the formula just explained.

Reading #13

COLONIAL WILLIAMSBURG

Colonial Williamsburg is the term popularly used to refer to the restoration and preservation of eighteenth-century Williamsburg, Virginia, that was begun many years ago. The Colonial Williamsburg Foundation is the corporate name of the organization that carries on the restoration, preservation, and related educational programs.

Colonial Williamsburg has an appeal for everyone in every season. Among these appeals are the many buildings furnished with outstanding English and American antiques, the colonial crafts program, the boxwood gardens, and the numerous cultural and educational activities. Most important, Williamsburg recalls to present and future generations the lasting concepts of American government and individual liberty that were developed there over two centuries ago.

Mark the following statements either True (T), False (F), or Not Mentioned (N).

1. Colonial Williamsburg is near Boston, Massachusetts. _____
2. The corporate name of the agency in charge is the Colonial Williamsburg Foundation. _____
3. Williamsburg is only open in the summer for the tourist season. _____
4. Colonial Williamsburg was originally funded by the Rockefeller Foundation. _____
5. Colonial Williamsburg is a restoration of eighteenth-century life in America. _____

Now calculate your reading speed.

Finishing time: _____
Starting time: =_____
Reading time: _____(seconds)

$$\frac{}{\text{Word Count}} \times 60 = \frac{}{\text{Total words}}$$

$$\frac{}{\text{Total words}} \div \frac{}{\text{seconds}} = \frac{}{\text{WPM}}$$

The exact word count is 114. When you time yourself and use the formula as shown, you will actually be coming up with an estimated word count. This will, however, give you a close enough approximation of your word count to enable you to quickly obtain some indication of your reading speed. The word count for that paragraph of 114 × 60 equals 6840 total words, which, divided by the number of seconds it took you to read the paragraph, equals your WPM.

PRACTICE CHANGING YOUR READING HABITS

A point of caution or advice about practicing is in order. Today we have many gadgets and machines that do a lot of work for us. These are convenient and save us time and energy, but they often lead people to believe in easy solutions. Every week on TV, mysterious crimes and monumental problems are miraculously solved in thirty minutes or less. This leads many people to believe there are ways of accomplishing goals without work or effort. That may be true for some things, but not many. In fact, I don't know many purposes that can be fulfilled without effort or energy. In general, the bigger the accomplishment, the bigger the expenditure of effort required. Speed reading falls into the category of learning that requires concentration and effort. Once mastered, however, only periodic use is necessary to keep it working. It's like a muscle that needs only regular exercise to stay in shape.

To change your reading habits, first look at your present reading patterns—your regressions, for example. Do you make many regressions? Do these help you to attain a good reading speed? Obviously they do not. But if you intend to improve, then you should make a plan that includes *positive* ingredients. A plan cannot be based on what you say you are *not* going to do. Instead, it should indicate what you *are* going to do. For example, if you say to yourself, "I'm not going to regress," then all you think of is regressing. A better method would be to say, "I'm going to keep going to the next phrase. I'm going to push on."

It is a little like dieting. If all you think of is not eating, then eating is still on your mind. You have to replace the negative thought with a positive one. In order to eliminate a bad habit, you have to do three things. First, become aware that the habit exists. Second, have the desire to change. Third, set up and practice doing the opposite of the negative habit: that is, your goal. Think about going forward instead of not regressing.

Your plan, whatever it is, must be small in terms of time and what you are going to accomplish. For example, you might set a plan of reading fast for one minute out of every fifteen. In terms of time, this plan is the opposite of "I'm going to speed read everything from now on." One aim is small and definite and accomplishable. The other is grandiose and sounds good but is seldom achievable in realistic terms. The small plan allows you to see daily success and receive positive reinforcement for your efforts as you progress. It allows you to feel good about yourself as you change your reading habits. The other plan is vague and provides few opportunities to realize daily positive reinforcement.

A specific plan is what is needed. You should know exactly what steps you are working on. Plans like "I'm going to be a good reader" are worthy but too vague. Set specific goals for your reading and what you expect to accomplish. You might set your goal as simply as "I'm going to read this page as fast as I can."

Good plans that ultimately change your reading habits are repetitive. Plan something you can do fairly often so that it becomes part of your new regular reading habits.

All these ingredients will help you to change your reading habits. When you practice your reading, don't try to work on too many concepts at one time. Single out one method and work on that until you feel comfortable with it. Then go to the next. You might want to use a *reading do-plan*. A do-plan is a specific positive reading action you can do each day that will improve your reading rate and comprehension. After a week or two of concentrating on the same tasks, you'll see how they become a natural part of your new reading habits. You've simply replaced your old reading style with a new one. After you've mastered some steps, you can add new ones. Concentrate on just a few, and concentrate on *positive, small, specific,* and *repetitive* aspects. Don't overwhelm yourself with too many steps.

Here's a sample do-plan from one of the students I had in class not too long ago. Susan is a young nursing supervisor who was swamped with lots of reading in her profession. She said the do-plan method helped her achieve definite goals each day.

DO-PLAN FOR SPEED READING

Daily Specific Activity to Improve My Reading	Mon.	Tues.	Wed.	Thur.	Fri.	Sat.	Sun.
Read two chapters in my new book with no regressions.	✓	✓	✓	✓	✓	✓	✓
Read for 3 minutes with no vocalization.	✓	✓	✓	✓	✓	✓	✓
Pushed to my highest reading rate at least two minutes each day.	✓	✓	✓	✓	✓	✓	✓

As you can see, her goal is placed on the left. It is small, very specific, positive, repetitive and can be accomplished in a very short time. Each day Susan achieved that goal she felt the positiveness of speed reading and her efforts seemed more worthwhile. It is with such methods that old habits are changed and new ones are built—in reading or in just about anything else you care to accomplish.

This do-plan method is also called the *short-range technique* because it doesn't take long to improve this way. You set aside time for practice each day and really go at it. You have a definite plan. You usually see progress right away. Practice is concentrated and follows a definite routine. You clear away all other distractions. You make that phone call or finish that task before devoting all your energies to reading and practicing the concepts as presented in this book. You really concentrate. The do-plan style of learning to speed read is similar to the method of swimmers you see on the beach who go rushing into the water with definite, planned movements. They jump right into things and get them over with.

Other people like to tiptoe into the water, come back out, and gradually work their way in again. They might repeat the process over and over until they're used to the water. They're using the *periodic method*. This takes a little longer in getting into the water and also in learning to speed read.

With the periodic method, one might, for example, master the technique of reducing or eliminating regressions, but that's all. The person puts this book away for a week or two, then comes back at it and gives it another go. This time, the person masters or concentrates on eye span. Then the same cycle is repeated: The reader quits reading improvement techniques for a while then returns three weeks later and works at reducing the number of fixations. This method of periodically picking away at improving one's reading will work; it just takes longer than jumping right into it and going at it all the way. In the end, the reader will usually wind up with the same skills. One route is simply shorter or more concentrated. It's all a matter of individual preference. The idea is that everyone gets into the water, and you can all get into speed reading, but you have to work at it. Pick a method and keep at it.

Now let's put theory into practice on a few paragraphs. Remember to make a conscious effort to go for speed. No regressions, keep going forward, read in phrases or thought units and with a good eye span, and don't rely on auditory methods. Remember, too, no physical movements. Trust in your new abilities and let your eyes fly over the material. Use the Progress Chart page in the back of the book to keep track of your progress.

Reading #14

SPORTS AND READING

Any good athlete will tell you he practiced long and hard to get in shape and achieve high honors. We seldom hear of any athlete becoming a champion without any effort. Do we expect to be able to run the hundred-yard dash without training? No, we consider training to be a part of the game. Once he is in shape, it is easier for an athlete to keep in condition. Reading skills develop the same way. Any person who can see words and has the desire can learn to read faster and with understanding.

Mark the following statements either True (T), False (F), or Not Mentioned (N).

1. Good athletes practice long and hard. _____
2. Learning to speed read takes practice. _____
3. Reading skills develop naturally. _____
4. We expect to be able to run the hundred-yard dash without training. _____
5. Anyone who can see and is motivated can improve his or her reading. _____

Time/Sec.	5	7	10	12	15	17	20	25
WPM	1212	866	606	505	404	356	303	242

If your time isn't shown, divide your time, in seconds, into 6060 for your exact WPM. (For answers, see page 151.)

Reading #15

HOLIDAY INNS

Holiday Inns are located all across America and can be found in every major city in the nation. The Holiday Inn philosophy, according to their advertisements, is simple. It is to give you the most important things when you travel. Their ads say only Holiday Inn gives you the widest choice of the most popular locations, wherever you travel. You can choose among a variety of locations in and around town. Or take your choice of locations throughout the suburbs or all along the highways. So you can be right where you want to be.

Next, they say everything in their hotels must measure up to their "no surprise" standards. Things you notice: For example, every mattress must be comfortable—specified *Manufacturer's Top of the Line*. Right down to things you might not notice, like cleaning your carpet every day. These are some of the reasons why Holiday Inns say they please more travelers than anybody else. They think they should be #1 in pleasing you.

Mark the following statements either True (T), False (F), or Not Mentioned (N).

1. Holiday Inns are found around the world. _____
2. The Holiday Inn philosophy is simple. _____
3. The Inns must measure up to "no surprise" standards. _____
4. The Holiday Inns were the first popular, nationwide family hotel chain in America. _____

5. The Holiday Inns think they should be #1 in pleasing you.

_____

Time/Sec.	7	10	12	15	20	25	30	35
WPM	1466	1026	855	684	513	410	342	293

If your time isn't shown, divide the number of seconds it took you to read the story into 10,260. That will give you your speed or WPM for the Progress Chart. (See page 151 for answers.)

Chapter 7

IMPROVING YOUR RECOGNITION RATE

Your *recognition rate* is the rate at which you see and understand what you read. A more technical definition for this term might be "the rate at which you see and understand the symbols on the printed page."

The process we generally refer to as reading is actually an interpreting-thinking process. Your recognition rate is one of the most basic factors that must be taken into account if you are going to be a speed reader, because a slow recognition rate usually results in a slow reading speed. We are assuming here that the reader has normal vision or is wearing some type of corrective lens to give normal vision. Fatigue is a common factor experienced by readers who have a slow recognition rate. For them, reading is a slow, sluggish, painful process. They get a headache or their eyes become tired or their vision grows blurred after twenty or thirty minutes of reading. Thus, readers with a slow recognition rate seldom sit down to read for any long periods of time. They can blame many things for their slow reading style, such as boring or dull subject matter, their limited vocabulary, eye strain, lack of concentration, or the mysterious sudden headaches they say they get when they read.

Sometimes the recognition rate is called the *word-response rate*. Another way to think about it is how fast you think or react to what you see. Sometimes it is called the *rate of perception*. In essence, it is how fast you recognize and process what you are reading. A slow recognition rate causes a slow reading speed. Staring at words on the page for several seconds lowers your WPM without increasing comprehension. In addition, slow recognition rate encourages regressions. A slow recognition rate, too many long fixations, and too many regressions can reduce speeds to extremely slow rates. Slow rates in turn have an effect on comprehension. These factors have nothing to do with IQ, motivation, or vocabulary.

You might ask how you are to learn new words and build a good vocabulary if you don't stop and examine new words? Vocabulary development is explored in chapter 8, but the point for this discussion is that, while your recognition rate may be slow for new words, it should not be slow on all the other words. Since most people know most of the words they read each day, recognition rate should not be a problem. The only reason it is a problem is that most people haven't worked at improving it. *You can train your recognition rate,* and that training will make you a faster and better reader.

An important point to keep in mind is that recognition rate is learned at a young age. It is very common for young children to stumble along with uncertainty in their reading, especially when new words are continually being introduced to them. Thus, it is easy to develop a slow recognition rate that is then applied to all words, new or old. Sometimes this problem is referred to as *lazy eyes,* but your eyes will be lazy only if you let them. If you are a fast reader, your recognition rate is rapid, with no long stares of uncertainty. During the recognition phase, you quickly and effortlessly recognize a word or group of words as well as immediately understand the meaning associated with the word(s). Because this process is so quick, your reading speed is very fast. Your comprehension or understanding is equally rapid. You read and comprehend quickly and with more understanding because your eyes and brain are instantly perceiving the author's message. Perhaps this whole process can be compared to a computer. Some computers process data faster than others. The accuracy of a new, fast computer is equal to that of an older, slower model; the difference is in the processing speed. Your mind is like a computer with fantastic potential. It has the ability to process words at amazing speed. You only have to feed it faster, and you do this by reading faster.

Let's check your recognition rate, or word-response rate, by using the following test. We can utilize the results to improve your reading abilities. It should also be pointed out that this test of recognition abilities has often been used to determine recognition rates for driving tests. Yes, your recognition rate has an effect on how well you drive, in that it is some indication of how quickly you react to what you see. The following test for driving tells whether your reaction speed qualifies you to drive over 45 mph. In the case of speed reading, it tells how your recognition rate compares to that of thousands of others who have taken the same test. The directions are simple: See how fast you can identify the twelve numerals in the twelve squares in the proper sequence, or numerical order. Touch each number with the index finger as you read it. Check your time in seconds. See how long it takes you to do this. Ready? Remember, you must touch each number in sequence. Go!

4	3	10	12
6	11	8	9
1	7	2	5

How did you come out? Within nine seconds? Your reactions and eye span are about average. Within seven seconds? Very good. Within six or five? Excellent! If your time was longer than nine seconds, your reactions are too slow, and you had better not drive over 45 mph. You should work at improving your recognition rate, which will improve your reading speed as well as enable you to react more quickly to unexpected driving factors such as those interstate highway signs that are so easy to miss. It is a slow recognition rate and too many fixations that cause people to miss those signs. If they had time, they could easily read them accurately and correctly. The frustration of a slow recognition rate is obvious when the driver says something to the effect: "Darn, I missed that sign. Did you see what it said? I couldn't finish it; I saw the name of the city, but how many miles was that?" Or maybe, "What route was that?" or, "How many miles was it to that exit?"

Now try it again. Time yourself again. Try it three times. What is your average time?

INCREASING THE RATE

An excellent way to increase visual perception is through drill on the mechanical aspects of quickly recognizing words on the page. This can be done with machines, which will be discussed in chapter 11, but right now probably the only reason your recognition rate isn't faster is because you've never seriously pushed it to be faster. You've told yourself that stepping up your recognition rate only results in confusion or lack of comprehension, so you should be satisfied with your present level. You've wanted to increase your reading speed but haven't known how. Well, now you do.

From now on, the only thing that can hold you back is your own failure to put forth the effort needed to break old habits and form new ones. You can change your recognition rate by pushing yourself to read faster. You can, in essence, develop new eye muscles or new eye patterns and rid yourself of lazy eyes. Just as in training for anything involving complex motor skills, such as athletics, it takes motivation, willpower, consistency, and practice. But perhaps the most important ingredient is desire. I can show you the techniques, but you have to put them to use, and that's where your motivation level comes in. How motivated are you? How much energy are you willing to put forth to improve your reading skills? A football coach I once knew said, "Nothing worthwhile ever comes cheap. You give a man something and it amounts to nothing. If the price is high, sometimes a youngster isn't willing to accept the price. Then you have to push him. But it has to be done. Each man has a much greater potential than he thinks he does."

You have to push yourself to excel. "Pushing" to change your recognition rate means that you consciously move right along. You force yourself to read faster. It is important when you first do this that you think about speed as well as what you are reading. If you forget about speed, you still stop reading fast because you will slip back into your old habit of reading at one slow, steady speed; and, if you don't think about what you are reading to some extent, your comprehension will be so poor you will get discouraged. Thus, you should concentrate first on going faster and second on what the author is saying.

Apply your new, faster recognition rate to the following paragraph and see what a difference it will make in your reading speed. Remember, go for *speed first, comprehension second!*

Reading #16

MAKING STRESS WORK FOR YOU

Despite its reputation, stress itself is neither bad nor good. It's a state of heightened function that allows you to cope with or adapt to change—change that, for whatever reason, you deem as different than that to which you are accustomed. The stress reaction is physiologically identical to your responses to fear or excitement—your heart pounds, your breathing quickens, your body pumps out adrenaline. In short, stress is energy and, channeled constructively, it can help you achieve far more than you ever dreamt possible. The key is channeling this energy release.

Mark the following statements either True (T), False (F), or Not Mentioned (N).

1. Stress is energy. _____
2. Stress energy cannot be useful or good. _____
3. If you channel stress, its energy can be helpful to energizing you to new heights of achievement. _____
4. Research on stress is conducted at the University of Pittsburgh. _____
5. Few people ever get over stress. _____

Time/Sec.	5	7	10	12
WPM	1212	866	606	505

If your time isn't shown, divide your time, in seconds, into 6060 for your WPM. For answers, check page 151.

VARYING THE RATE

Another technique that is essential to speed reading is *varying the rate of speed*. The following example illustrates how varying your reading speed can greatly increase your words per minute. You could probably state fairly accurately how far you drive your car in one year. But could you state how far you "drive" your eyes during your reading activities in a year's time? Probably not. The chances are that your eyes travel about 1,600 feet per day in the reading process! That figure, which applies to most adults, amounts to approximately 584,000 feet per year—about 110 miles or 177 kilometers. If you are a high-school, college, or graduate student, these figures could easily be more than doubled.

Could you imagine traveling 110 or 220 miles in a car at one slow, constant speed? Or traveling 110 miles at, say, 20 miles per hour, with periodic long stops between exits and frequent backing up as you travel along trying to make your way to another city? Ridiculous, you might say. Yes—but that's the way some people read, and their goal is similar to driving a car: Their objective is to get to a predetermined point. The driver's goal may be a distant city or another state, while the reader's goal is to finish a page or a chapter. Both the driver and the reader need to push forward at varying rates according to the circumstances and conditions they face.

The point is that readers should vary their reading speed just as people do when they drive at different rates of speed. Reading speed should be geared to different variables, such as the purpose in reading the particular selection, the level of difficulty of the selection, the type and style of the author and text, and the familiarity of the material. Varying the rate of speed in reading allows you to be more selective in the application of your energies to the words. Why apply your energy in an equal fashion to all words? Ask yourself if each word is of equal value in its meaning. Is each word of equal importance in its relationship to the message of the author? Obviously not. So then a reader's energies should be applied proportionately.

Increased mental alertness, an overall higher average reading speed, and better comprehension are by-products of varying the rate of your reading speed. In achieving this goal, do not become "hung up," as many readers do, on only reading in horizontal line patterns. Develop some rapid vertical eye movements in your reading process just as in reading the front page of a newspaper. Get into the author's style, purpose, and format. Allow your eyes to flow ahead or scan the page before and after you read it. Pick up key words and lead sentences. Look for *go-ahead signals* that can help speed up your reading. Words such as "for example," and "for instance" indicate to the reader that similar or substantiating thoughts are about to follow. If you already understand the author's thought, you may want to skip the example. *Caution signals* like "however," "but," "although," and "on the other hand" should indicate a reduction in the reader's speed—or at least that some increased concentration is due on the point that is about to follow. These go-ahead signs and caution signals indicate the thought pattern of the writer, and you would do well to heed them.

The eyes are really servants of the mind and should do its bidding in the reading process, just as the hands do the bidding of the mind when told to "throw the ball" or "pick up the book." You can work on the process of varying the reading rate as you read any material. It is applicable to all levels of reading, from highly technical material to easy leisure reading.

What does varying the rate of speed actually do? It: (1) increases mental awareness, (2) utilizes energy in a more efficient manner, (3) places concentration power where it is needed, (4) increases overall reading speed, and (5) helps to build and maintain better comprehension levels.

When one varies the rate, some material is read faster and some material slower. The net result is: (1) a faster rate of speed and (2) concentration used where it is needed rather than focused equally on every word.

Thus, any chart showing a varied rate, such as this one,

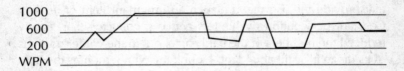

could represent a reader's rates over five to ten minutes of reading. By simply eyeballing the above chart, one can see that the average would be about 600–700 WPM. Compare this to the normal reader, whose steady, constant speed is usually slow—about 200 WPM—and can be graphically shown like this:

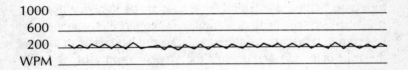

The first reader's rate is about 600–700 WPM in contrast to the second reader's 200 WPM. The net difference: The first reader is three times faster on the same material.

Let's utilize the technique of varying the rate on a lengthy story and see what it does to your words per minute. Read the article twice. The first time read it at your normal rate, keeping track of the number of seconds it takes you to read the selection. The second time, vary the rate. Hit your very highest and fastest rate and hold it up there for a while. Keep track of the number of seconds it takes you to complete this second reading. Then compare the two rates and see what a difference this new skill makes. Your comprehension should be outstanding because you're focusing on the important words and key phrases. Give it a try now. Go!

THE AMERICAN EAGLE

The American bald eagle was once abundant throughout the southwestern United States where there are large bodies of water that provide the fish that are such an important item of its diet. Constant persecution by hunters and egg collectors has greatly reduced the numbers of the bald eagle, but in the wilder portions of its range it is still abundant. During the winter months the bald eagle is even seen near New York City, though probably it does not breed within many miles of there. It now enjoys the full protection of the law and seems to be slowly increasing its numbers.

The bald eagle is most adept at the capture of fish. At times it may take its prey in a spectacular swoop from the blue; at other times it may be seen wading in shallow water, watchful for venturesome victims. But skillful though it may be in plying its trade, it is no match for that consummate fisherman the osprey eagle. It is common practice for the more powerful bald eagle to assume the role of bandit and to rob the weaker osprey of its catch. Having watched a successful dive on the part of its rival, the eagle rushes to the attack with a great show of fierceness. This alarms the osprey so that in order to make certain of escaping its tormentor, it releases its clutch on its burden and speeds away on frightened wings. The pirate is then free to seize the fish as it falls or to retrieve it at leisure from the surface of the water.

Fish do not form the sole diet of the bald eagle. When necessity arises, it is surprisingly swift on the wing, and in localities where wild ducks are abundant the eagle is perfectly capable of capturing them in full flight. Small mammals or rodents are also taken on occasion.

In flight the bald eagle is truly magnificent. With wings spread wide, floating with hardly perceptible efforts, it glides through the air with an ease and grace that no manmade machine has ever equaled. Aided by favorable air currents, it rises to tremendous heights, swinging in great circles, often beyond the vision of the human eye.

A few years ago, I had a remarkable view of the grandiosity of the bald eagle in flight. Driving along a turnpike in Pennsylvania, I suddenly spotted a moving spot of white. And there, sailing smoothly on outstretched wings, in full regalia of pure white head and tail, was the superb American bald eagle. His nearly motionless ease gave a false impression of his speed; for while I gazed spellbound he passed out of sight. The rays of reflected sunlight scintillated from his outstretched wings.

A national wildlife study showed that in one recent year there were 500 bald eagles born in the United States, and, of these, four were born in my native state of Ohio. Let's do our share to help preserve these birds as part of our heritage and do our part in the conservation of nature.

Dividing your time (seconds) into 39,000 will give you your WPM. You should be faster on this reading than any reading completed yet (if you truly varied your reading rate and did not slip back into the old habit of reading word by word at one slow, steady speed). You are breaking some lifetime habits and it may take a while; you just have to remember to keep at it.

Before we leave this chapter, let's apply varying the rate to the following paragraph.

Reading #17

THE QUARTERBACK

Why does the quarterback wait so long to throw a pass? A quarterback is considered really tough if he waits a long time in the pocket, with the defenders all around, pushing and shoving to get at him. He isn't showing he's tough or playing coy; he is just waiting for his receivers to get free downfield. Considering that defensive players are usually a lot bigger than a quarterback, it is understandable if he can't always "tough it out" in the pocket and ends up throwing a few passes too early.

If defense breaks through to the pocket, the quarterback may rush around wildly, dodging defenders and would-be tacklers, looking frantically for a pass receiver or a way to run down the field. This is called scrambling. "Scrambling with a purpose" when organized is called a "roll out." If all else fails, the quarterback usually finds himself on the bottom of a pile of defensive linemen. Now see why it's better to throw the ball as soon as possible?

Mark the following statements either True (T), False (F), or Not Mentioned (N).

1. Quarterbacks like to see how long they can stay in the pocket. _____

2. Quarterbacks in the NFL are exceptionally talented. _____
3. Scrambling with a purpose is sometimes called a "roll out." _____

4. Defensive linemen are usually a lot bigger than quarterbacks. _____

5. The Pittsburgh Steelers are the all-time Super Bowl champions. _____

Time/Sec.	7	10	12	15	17	20	25
WPM	1474	1032	860	688	607	516	413

If your time isn't shown, divide your time, in seconds, into 10,320 for your WPM. Don't forget to keep all your progress recorded in the back of the book. For answers to the quiz, see page 151.

Chapter 8

BETTER COMPREHENSION, GREATER RETENTION

Comprehension is the art of understanding what you read. Retention is what you retain or remember from that initial understanding.

Because it is so unlike speed, which can basically be attributed to eye movements, comprehension is probably the most misunderstood aspect of reading. Eye patterns can be seen, studied, and understood. They are visible. Comprehension, on the other hand, is invisible and is sometimes thought to be mysterious. You can't trace or see it. Even definitions and explanations of comprehension often disagree.

In my opinion, comprehension is simply the understanding we receive when we read something.

Understanding is the second half of the reading process; speed, or rate, is the first half. We learn to move our eyes over the printed page in a certain way; the result is meaning. If you don't move your eyes properly, you reduce your comprehension. Thus, rate is the first essential factor; comprehension comes next, as the product of this effort. Comprehension doesn't have to be mysterious. And it can be improved if you go about it properly.

Comprehension in reading can be compared to accuracy in typing or style in swimming. In the development of all three of these skills, you must first get the speed where you want it and then work on fine points of accuracy, style, or comprehension, as the case may be. If you're trying to be a good typist, you push your speed up until you are satisfied, and then you work on accuracy. In swimming, you first get to the other end of the pool in the time desired, then you begin to concentrate on improving style, stroke, or positioning of the head, shoulders, etc. Likewise with reading, which brings us to the basic question of this chapter: *How can comprehension be improved?* Here are the steps you should incorporate into your reading if you are to develop outstanding comprehension skills.

First, *attention* is an absolute prerequisite to intensive mental impressions. Impressions from the printed page are the essence of comprehension. In fact, the intensity of the original impression is proportionate to the attention given the item to be remembered. In other words, the more attention you pay to something, the stronger the mental impression you will receive.

What is attention? It is the will to direct the intellect into some particular channel and keep it there. It is mind over matter. What does that mean to you in terms of improving your ability to remember what you read? It means that you must give your undivided attention to what you want to recall. You must *will* yourself to fix vividly in your subconscious mind whatever you mean to remember. Your memory awaits your commands. The human mind is a powerhouse of untapped energy.

The next factor is *interest*. Interest is very important. We always give voluntary attention to anything we are interested in. A musician may give a lot of attention to a musical rendition by a great master but may have great difficulty in giving

chain of related ideas helps to recall the others that belong with it. Thus, the person who is trying to recall has several "handles" to take hold of in calling forth any set of related facts or ideas that he has impressed upon his mind through previous reading. For example, summer: swimming, sunbathing, vacations, picnics, golf, heat, barbecues, Fourth of July. Another example would be war: guns, uniforms, battles, rations, planes, jeeps, ships, tanks. The reader associates one word with another or with a series of other words, in accordance with his or her experience.

Repetition is another technique that improves comprehension. Briefly stated: All other things being equal, the intensity of an impression can be increased by repeatedly reviewing it. Studies on comprehension show that the first time a person reads something his comprehension usually ranges from 40 to 60 percent. The second time he reads the same material, there is a significant increase in comprehension. And the third time he reads the same material there is still some further increase in comprehension.

Distributed practice is highly effective in improving comprehension when it is properly coupled with repetition. Experiments have shown that you are much more likely to recall what you have studied again and again if you study at *spaced intervals* rather than performing the second reading immediately following the first. That is why it is suggested that you begin preparing for a test several weeks ahead of the actual examination and study the same subject repeatedly at different intervals.

The use of several different approaches provides a multitude of avenues to improving your memory and comprehension skills. In studying difficult material for the first time or in reviewing for exams, just *reading* is not enough. You need to do more than cover the pages in the usual way. *Write* the subject matter down in outline form; make a summary or compile an organized list. *Say* it aloud. *Underline* the important passages.

Write *notes* on the margin of the book. *Draw* diagrams or sketches to illustrate it. *Make up a test* of your own on the material, and later *take the test* you have made. The more things you do with the subject matter, the better your recall will be.

You will improve your ability to comprehend and retain what you have read if you follow the "Reading Power" rules outlined on page 97.

Apply these principles of better comprehension to the following paragraph and watch the results! Use the Progress Chart in the back to record your improvement.

Reading #18

BEST RUNNING BACK IN THE NFL?

Who's the best running back in the National Football League today? Some people might choose Eric Dickerson of the Indianapolis Colts or Roger Craig of the San Francisco Forty-Niners. Both of them have helped their teams win in two important ways: They're powerful ball carriers and dependable pass receivers.

Even so, the player who gained the most yards by running the ball and catching passes in two recent seasons is Herschel Walker. In 1987 and 1988, this recently traded player gained a total of 3625 yards for the Dallas Cowboys. That's more than two miles! Herschel also led the NFL last year in rushing. Who's the best running back in the NFL? Hard to say, but Herschel Walker's running statistics lead the pack.

Mark the following statements either True (T), False (F), or Not Mentioned (N).

1. In two recent seasons, Herschel Walker led the NFL in statistics. _____

2. Herschel Walker was recently traded. _____
3. His ball-carrying statistics in two recent seasons, 1987 and 1988, have been for the Dallas Cowboys. _____
4. The Forty-Niners and Colts also have outstanding running backs. _____
5. The Steelers have won more Super Bowls than any other team. _____

Time/Sec.	5	7	10	12	15	17	20
WPM	1572	1123	786	655	524	462	393

If your time isn't shown, divide your time, in seconds, into 7860 for your WPM.

VOCABULARY

An old argument often heard when it comes to the study of comprehension relates to vocabulary. You've probably heard the case before; it goes something like this: "I don't understand what I read because my vocabulary isn't big enough," or "I didn't know that word, that's why I didn't understand the paragraph" or that article or page or sentence, and, "Once I build up my vocabulary, I'm going to start to read." The excuses go on ad infinitum.

The truth is that no one understands *exactly* what a writer is saying with each and every word. Words have a general meaning, and we understand generally what the author is trying to convey to us. Do you doubt that words usually have a general meaning for most readers? Many lawyers make a living out of debating what certain words really mean or connote. If all words meant the same thing to all people, communication would be much easier than it is.

The best thing to do for reading ability is to read. A good vocabulary isn't built overnight, and you don't learn to read by building the vocabulary first and then learning to read faster later. You'll wind up waiting forever if you use that logic. A good vocabulary is the result of reading, not vice versa. So if you want a large vocabulary, start to read and keep at it. You'll soon develop a bigger and better vocabulary.

EYE MOVEMENTS AND COMPREHENSION

Up to now, you have learned a great deal about the eye movements made in reading. Our emphasis has been on ways to improve these movements. You may have read or heard that this kind of approach causes a loss in comprehension; the argument basically goes like this: Poor eye movements are a result of poor reading, and if we read better our eye movements will be better. This is like telling a man that he'll be a better husband and father if he gets along with his wife and kids. That kind of thinking doesn't tell the husband what he should do specifically to be a better husband or father. Advice givers who think like this would probably respond, "We told you that you should be a better husband—or a better reader. Now you figure it out."

People need to be told specific techniques on how to be better readers (or better partners). If we really want someone to learn something, we show them by examples and concrete, step-by-step methods. That's basically what this book does when it demonstrates techniques like a good, wide eye-span, no regressions, short fixations, etc. Compare this kind of specific know-how to advice like "read faster."

What's more, this whole debate—speed versus comprehension—is really a moot point, for comprehension initially always lags behind when any change is made in one's reading style. The mind has to readjust to the tempo at which it is being fed information. It is used to receiving, sorting, and interpreting data at a certain rate of speed. Any sudden change means the mind has to reacclimate to receiving data at a new faster rate. We call this factor *comprehension lag*. In the field of speed reading, it usually takes ten to fifteen days for the mind to acclimate to the new reading rate. It is virtually impossible to improve the reading speed and the comprehension at the same time. One must come first. The lag process worked like this for one reader:

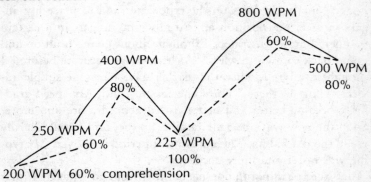

The reader started at 200 WPM with 60 percent comprehension. After practice over several weeks, he was able to read at 500 WPM with 80 percent comprehension. Once the mind adjusts to the new rate at which data is fed to it, along with the increased concentration applied, comprehension is better than ever.

Comprehension is dependent on a host of variables, such as the level of difficulty of the material being read, the purpose in reading the material, the speed at which it is being read and how new that level of speed is to the reader, and the reader's physiological and psychological condition. If the reader's mind has experienced the feeling of reading at that speed before and has grown fairly comfortable with it, then comprehension will be better than ever. Practice is needed for ten to fifteen days while one changes old habits and learns new ones.

Learning to speed read is very much like learning to type.

The goal of both is speed and accuracy. I once took a typing course. I knew how to type before I took the class, and when the teacher told me I couldn't use my hunt-and-peck method, which was accurate but very slow, my typing was suddenly worse. I was trying to do what the teacher was asking of me, but I made more errors than ever before, and my speed wasn't as good as with my hunt-and-peck system. I was being taught not to look at the keys on the typewriter and to place my fingers in a certain position and to move my fingers in a certain manner. I grew frustrated. I thought about giving it all up and going back to my old ways. "At least I was accurate before," I thought to myself. Then the teacher gave me some simple advice: "Hang in there." For some reason I did. My speed gradually became better and better as I practiced more and more. Soon the new ways became familiar to me, and I could hardly recall the old habits. The adjustment period was over. My typing was faster and more accurate.

In speed reading, the sequence works the same way. At first you think your accuracy or comprehension is worse than ever, and you debate whether or not you should continue with your efforts to master this new skill. It is easy to give in to temptation and talk yourself into being satisfied with slow speed in reading. The techniques being taught to you through this book are new to you. Give them a chance. Practice them. The end result will be a better reading rate and much more comprehension! Just remember and compare the process to learning to type. Relearning a skill is always harder than learning it the first time. Changing how you read is harder than learning to read for the first time. This is so because you have to *unlearn* the old ways in order to learn the new.

Another argument about comprehension says that if you concentrate on specific techniques (no matter what techniques they are), you will give most or all of your attention to those techniques instead of concentrating on the author's message. If you examine that logic closely, you'll see it's like telling an athlete to forget working and practicing on all the specific techniques taught by the coach and just think about being a superstar. Teams and individuals succeed and excel because they pay a great deal of attention to the little mechanics, steps, and procedures. They work at them over and over again until they master them completely. That's what being a professional means. So it is with reading. This book tells you the specifics. It gives you precise techniques that will make you a better reader: for example, *shorten your fixation time, broaden your eye span, read in thought units, don't regress, always push forward, vary the rate, quicken your recognition rate,* etc.

You know as well as I do, and common sense dictates, that to speed read or to improve your reading takes more than the mere desire to pick up a book and read better and faster. It is through actual step-by-step methods and hours of practice that people master anything in life. It is through such specifics and hard work that success and concentration are achieved. These ingredients are necessary for any worthwhile accomplishment.

The formula I am prescribing works like this:

$$RR = MC = MC = MR$$

The letters in the formula above stand for:

Rapid Reading	=	More Concentration	=	More Comprehension	=	More Retention

Here's the logic. If you start with step 1 (rapid reading) you are forced to concentrate and pay attention. You have no time to daydream and let your mind wander. You are reading a little faster than your normal slow rate, and this leads to step 2— more concentration. You are forced to concentrate more because you are reading faster. Simple, but true. Step 3—more concentration means more comprehension! After all, isn't this what people say: "If I could only concentrate more, I'd get more out of what I read." Thus, if a reader concentrates more, it is logical that he will retain more, which is the fourth step. The formula can be summarized like this: You learn the specific steps of fast reading and thus begin to read faster; the increased rate makes you more attentive and you concentrate more; the greater concentration is rewarded by better comprehension; the better comprehension in turn gives you more retention.

Don't let comprehension be a roadblock for you. There are certain obstacles that hinder reading speed. We know how to correct these, and you can already see the results of your efforts. Continue concentrating on learning the specific steps, and you'll see your reading speed and comprehension both improve. Check your progress to date in the back of the book as proof of your newfound success.

Try these next two paragraphs and remember . . . *speed* . . . *speed!*

Reading #19

READING SPEED'S EFFECT ON COMPREHENSION

Some people believe that if they read too fast their comprehension will suffer. However, research shows that as you learn to read rapidly, comprehension may be even better than it was before. Such improvement generally is attributed to the fact that the more rapidly you read, the more you must concentrate on what is being read. Therefore, you comprehend more. Comprehension may be lower for a short time when you first attempt to speed read, but comprehension almost always improves when speed is gained.

Mark the following statements either True (T), False (F), or Not Mentioned (N).

1. Comprehension may suffer when you first attempt speed reading. _____
2. Poor vision is a factor to be considered when learning to speed read. _____
3. Comprehension improves when speed is gained. _____
4. Skipping, scanning and skimming are techniques used in speed reading. _____
5. One reason why comprehension improves when speed is gained is increased concentration. _____

Time/Sec.	3	5	7	10	12
WPM	1840	1104	789	552	460

If your time isn't shown, divide your time, in seconds, into 5520 for your WPM. (For answers, see page 151.)

Reading #20

CELLULAR PHONES

The cellular phone is fast becoming a standard business tool all over the world. Cellular phone users are increasing at a rate of 10,000 or more each month. It is estimated that 10 million of these phones will be in use in the United States by the turn of the century.

Just a few years ago, the price tag for one of these phones was over $1,000, but now the price is down to about half of that. Lower prices and advanced technology that has improved the quality in these phones have generated a greater demand. Maybe now more than ever, you can truly be "just a phone call away."

Mark the following statements either True (T), False (F), or Not Mentioned (N).

1. Cellular phones are becoming standard business equipment.
   _____

2. Very few people today have cellular phones. _____
3. The price of a cellular phone continues to drop. _____
4. AT&T leads the field in cellular phone technology. _____
5. There will be about 10,000,000 cellular phones in use by the year 2000. _____

Time/Sec.	3	4	5	7	10	12
WPM	2240	1680	1344	960	672	560

If your time isn't shown, divide your time, in seconds, into 6720 for your WPM.

READING POWER

KNOW EXACTLY WHY

you are reading a story. Ask yourself what you want from the material.

ASSOCIATE

new ideas with old ones or with your experience.

REPETITION

Read the material at least twice. Then read it once again.

LOOK FOR KEY WORDS,

take notes, and use other approaches (underlining, outlining, saying key words aloud, etc.). The more you use, the more your comprehension will increase.

CONCENTRATION AND ATTENTION

Focus on what you're reading, not on the radio or surrounding events or daydreams, etc.

DISTRIBUTED PRACTICE

Read the same material at different intervals, allowing some time to lapse between each reading.

The ultimate purpose of reading is to synthesize the author's thoughts and your thinking, so

ANALYZE AND USE

what you've learned or read as soon as you've finished. This can be accomplished by putting the author's message into your own words, reflecting upon what you've read, and evaluating what the author said.

Chapter 9

OVERCOMING THE MAJOR OBSTACLES TO SPEED READING

You have now completed eight chapters of this book and through them you've become a better reader. You have improved your reading skills, habits, and attitudes. You are much more knowledgeable about reading and your own reading abilities. You've learned to determine what your reading needs are and how to meet them. You've learned how your reading skills compare with others of comparable or similar educational background. You've learned to read faster and faster. You've learned to improve your comprehension. You've learned to become a balanced reader, able to apply different reading skills to different reading situations.

You have measured many of your new reading gains. The tests you've taken on the various readings show your reading speed and comprehension and actually demonstrate your progress. But no matter how great your reading progress has been, you can surely continue to make further gains. How to do this now becomes the question. You might ask, how have others done it? How have others continued to improve? Or maybe the question should be put another way: What has kept them from achieving the high reading speeds they desire? After almost thirty years of teaching speed reading, I've concluded there are eight major reasons why many people don't achieve the high reading skills they desire.

1. Limited Eye Span. Some people see single letters instead of whole words when they read. Their eye span is so small that they don't even read one word at a time. Obviously, their reading speed goes along at a snail's pace. In order to read faster, they must master the eye-span technique, for this is the primary determinant in controlling their reading rate or potential. Most people can read at least one word at a time, so for them reading faster is a matter of increasing the eye span from one word to two words at a single glance. From two words, their eye span can go to three or four or five, depending on motivation, amount of practice, etc. Some people are critical of reading like this and claim that such fast reading automatically means poor reading. This is not true. If the reading process is such that the reader is more efficient, finishes a selection faster and more easily, and comprehends more (or even the same amount) at a higher rate of speed, who is to say that is poor reading? In fact, it is generally true that the slow readers are less sure about the meaning of what they are reading than the fast readers. It is slower readers who generally have reading problems until they master these skills.

Research has shown distinctly (and beyond debate) exactly how the eyes move in reading. It is up to us to utilize these modern findings to improve our eye movements in the reading process. It is essential that you understand how and why the eyes move in the manner they do in order to read. That's what this book has been showing you. Your mind and your eyes can take in more than one word at a glance. Many people are held back only by their habit of a limited eye span. They have read one word at a time for so long that it is difficult for them to change. That's where practice and patience comes in. People can change—if they want to. Motivation and desire, along with the steps presented in this book, are the keys to better and faster reading.

2. Regressing. Re-tracing or re-reading is a time-consuming factor that burns up WPM and slows the reader down, sometimes almost to a halt. It's like trying to win the Indianapolis 500 on race day with the driving style of backing up every other lap. Ridiculous, right? How can speed be attained if the driver backs up in the race or the reader goes backward over the material? Speed is obviously forward motion or, more precisely, rapid forward movement. Any backward movements serve to impede or reduce that speed. Of all the time-consuming factors, regression is the most commonly reported by people in my classes, yet, of all the speed-reading techniques, the easiest to master is eliminating regressions. And readers see immediate improvement after doing so.

A most important question is whether you want to regress or whether you regress from habit. Many times people go back over material and re-read words because they feel more comfortable doing that. It gives them a sense of security and the impression that they are comprehending more. They psych themselves into believing that they re-read words because it is good for them. They claim that they sacrifice speed for comprehension. The truth is, many people regress simply because it is a habit. Poor eyesight may be a valid cause for regression. A poor vocabulary may be another. But these reasons are not applicable to most people. This is not to say all of us do not regress now and then. However, regressions should be few and far between. Controlling regressions is critical if you are to become a speed reader.

3. Subvocalizing. Reliance upon hearing the words mentally causes many readers not to read as fast as they want to. They're slowed down by waiting to hear the words mentally. They subvocalize their way through a book. This reliance creates an artificial roadblock or barrier to a rapid, flexible reading rate.

It is usually the result of the way the reader was taught to read as a child and is the carryover effect of still hearing the words, even though this is no longer necessary. It is not uncommon for students to use subvocalizing when they study or when they are confronted by a tough test. When the chips are down, many people "kick in" the extra senses (such as hearing by subvocalizing) in order to get through difficult material. That doesn't mean, however, that comprehension is any better because one hears the words or doesn't hear them for that matter. The question is really, what does relying on hearing words do to speed? And the obvious answer is that it slows it down.

4. Reading Everything at the Same Speed. This is probably the most commonly misunderstood aspect of reading. Most people were taught to read at one steady rate, and they subsequently apply this rate to all reading, with few exceptions. They read novels at the same rate they read newspapers. Or they read the newspaper at the same rate they read their insurance policy. In almost every elementary school I've seen, the emphasis is on teaching the child to read and not on rates of speed. Once the child is taught the mechanics of the reading process in the first and second grades, the next three years are spent building vocabulary. Very little or no effort is ever put into developing the child's reading rate. This may not be true in all schools, but I believe it to be the case in most.

People later on take speed-reading courses, and their goal is to be able to read *everything* at some remarkable new rate. In essence, they plan to cash in their old slow, steady rate for one new rapid, steady rate. This isn't what speed reading is all about. Let's compare the process to walking and running. Most people walk. Perhaps for some the goal is to walk faster or maybe run at a high rate of speed. They can learn to walk faster—how much faster depends on factors such as those we've explained in this book: practice, technique, motivation, physiological conditions, etc. But even those who get to be extremely fast runners can't maintain that rate for long. They usually wind up with varying rates based on a variety of factors. Such is the case in speed reading. The key is to vary the rate and not to read everything at one steady speed—fast or slow.

We might also compare reading to traveling in a car. If your goal is to go from Pittsburgh to Miami, varying conditions along the way demand varying speeds. No one would buy or want a car that goes only at one speed. Reading should be like driving—flexible, adaptable, and purposeful.

5. Poor Concentration. I often hear statements like this: "If I could only concentrate, I'd get good grades" or "If I could concentrate, I could read faster, but I get tired easily. I guess my attention span is too short." A businessman once said to me, "I'd give a thousand dollars to learn to keep my mind on what I am reading. I'm often aware that I have not been paying attention. I think about a multitude of things when I read. I watch others around me. I look away from the book. Look back. Try to find my place again. Read a little bit more. Daydream for a while. Think about other things. Then read some more. Pretty soon I'm bored. I figure my concentration is bad. I see others who sit for hours and don't move and just read. I wish I could do that."

This kind of experience is common. It happens to everyone at one time or another. But you can learn to concentrate if you realize that poor concentration is one of your reading problems. The fallacy about concentration is that many people think it can be overcome by regressing or making long fixations or reading slowly. What these people fail to realize is that a moderate or fast rate of speed forces us to pay attention. It's when we read slowly that our minds have time to daydream and wander. If they're in a hurry to get somewhere and get a job done, most people don't fool around—they go right about accomplishing the task. It's the person who sees no time factor or no purpose in a task who is slow, dreamy, indifferent, and lacks the power of concentration. Fast readers are usually good readers. Slow readers are often poor readers. Not always, but often.

Speed and comprehension skills go together like bread and butter. They can't be isolated. As you increase your reading speed, you increase your ability to comprehend. You're actually comprehending faster—and usually in greater amounts because you are concentrating more. With greater reading speed, you cover more material, get more ideas, grasp more thoughts, gain a broader understanding, and retain more—all in the given amount of time. If you had that same amount of time and just browsed through the book, how would the results (speed and comprehension) compare?

6. *Reading Every Word Unnecessarily.* The reverence for the printed word is awesome. Many people don't dare to skip a word or phrase or sentence because they would feel guilty. Or they would feel they had missed something. This is truly a delusion. Every word printed or said is not of equal importance, and it is an unwise use of human talent and energy to apply them equally to every word. Tests have demonstrated that when we listen to another person speaking, we do not hear each and every word. We hear the words we need to hear. In essence, we hear a thought stream. In reading, the same phenomenon is possible. You can train yourself to read by seeing merely the words you need to see. Moreover, when reading fast, you may find you are as close to the writer's stream of thought as if you were trying to read each word. Unimportant words get in the way and slow you down.

Most authors never mean their readers to hang on every word in every sentence in every paragraph on every page. When you have finished this book will you remember all the words? Obviously not. Can you remember every word of every conversation you've had today? Obviously not. People have to learn the skill of applying selective hearing and selective listening and *selective reading.* That isn't to be confused with hearing only what you want to hear or reading into material only what you want to find. It is the process of accurately and quickly, with a minimum amount of effort, tuning into the message another person is trying to convey.

7. Lack of Drive. Some people are slow readers simply because they don't force themselves to read faster or break old habits. It's easier to just go along and settle for less. It's like Sally, who came to my classes and after the first lesson said, "You know what my problem is? I need to wear glasses. I have 'em at home, but I'm too lazy to wear 'em. They're a pain. I'm always losing them, anyhow."

I've purposefully avoided discussions in this book about poor vision or mental or emotional blocks to reading because I've made what I think are some very basic assumptions about people . . . such as that if Sally took care of her poor vision, she could master the techniques recommended. I've assumed that if other students would stop fighting their desire to improve their reading, they too could master the steps shown in this book. I've assumed that this book is for readers, like you, who have the will, the ability, and the determination to accept these concepts, apply them to their own reading styles, and emerge as better, faster, and stronger readers.

There is no easy answer for lack of drive. The bottom line is and has to be—*it's up to you.* I can only show you how to speed read. You have to have the energy and the physiological and mental ability to make the eyes and brain work in the manner described in this book. The average person can do it.

8. Overconcern with Comprehension. Everybody wants to read at a zillion words per minute or some such fantastic rate that they deem applicable to their self-concept. There's nothing wrong with that. The only problem is that many people want to learn to do this without any effect on their comprehension rate—up or down, good or bad, better or worse. You might take exception to the first statement, "Everybody wants to . . ."

But let's look at America in general. We now live in a society where there is a great emphasis on speed: It's commonly believed that fast cars are better than slow cars; fast-food stores are extremely popular because they're fast; there's an express checkout in the grocery store for people in a hurry; fast typists are held in high esteem. Taking a short course, mastering a skill in a hurry, completing the job quickly, reading fast—the examples go on and on. The fact is, we now live in a society where there is a premium on speed.

Yet it must be recognized that learning to read fast can be done easily, but not without some effect on the rate of comprehension. That effect can be temporary or permanent, depending on the individual and a whole host of other variables. In teaching people to speed read, however, I have found that too many people spend so much time thinking about their comprehension that their energies for better reading skills are thwarted. Maybe it is a matter of priorities.

In learning speed reading, speed has to come first. Once speed is established, practice will bring comprehension and accuracy. It is a matter of acclimation. Some people don't have what it takes to hang in there long enough. Their obvious immediate reaction is to drop the speed back again, which restores the comprehension because the brain is used to functioning at that lower speed. So the cycle starts and repeats itself over and over again. Speed is not attained because comprehension lags. Comprehension is calling the shots. This is unfortunate, for all one needs to do is practice and bear with the new reading speed and, above all, vary the rate. Comprehension will soon be established as the mind adjusts to receiving data at a new faster rate. Once that is done, in fact, comprehension is usually better than ever, for as was said earlier, there is less time for irrelevant thought processes when the mind must deal with data coming in rapidly.

* * *

The eight factors just discussed have caused some people to fall short of their reading expectations. On the other hand, more people have gone on to achieve the speed and comprehension they want. They are well satisfied with their newfound reading skills. There is no age restriction on success in reading. Records are made to be broken. With the aid of modern methods, reading has been refined to a skill anyone who is predisposed to can master. Remember, you don't have to regress! You can vary the rate and read faster than ever! You can zoom right through the material!

Try the next three exercises and record your time on the Progress Chart on page 149.

Reading #21

UP IN SMOKE

Attitudes about cigarette smoking are changing. According to the U.S. National Center for Disease Control, only about one out of four adults in the U.S. now smokes. That's the smallest percentage of smokers in the U.S. since the Surgeon General announced the link between smoking and cancer in 1964.

Why? Most likely because the mounting evidence that links the dangers of smoking to both the smoker and the "side stream" smoking effects to nearby nonsmokers. Bans and instructions on smoking are ever increasing. In the U.S., 41 states now restrict smoking in public places. No doubt about it, the image of smoking has drastically changed since Humphrey Bogart first lit up. Even TV stars today like Don Johnson, who are often shown with a cigarette, do not actually light up. Cigarette smoking just may be going up in smoke.

Answer the following questions either True (T), False (F), or Not Mentioned (N):

1. Attitudes in the U.S. about cigarette smoking are changing. _____

2. Today only one out of four adults are smokers. _____
3. TV star Don Johnson, often shown with a cigarette, doesn't light up. _____
4. Mounting evidence shows a link between cancer and smoking. _____
5. Forty-five of the fifty states now restrict smoking in public places. _____

Time/Sec.	3	5	7	10	12	15
WPM	2880	1728	1234	864	720	576

If your speed isn't shown, divide your time, in seconds, into 8640 for your WPM. Compare it with your first reading in terms of both WPM and comprehension.

Reading #22

THE PERFECT GAME

Don Larsen pitched in the major leagues from 1953 to 1967, but he was never known as an outstanding pitcher. In fact, his record was 81 wins and 91 loses. But on October 8, 1956, Larsen did something no other pitcher has ever done. He pitched a "perfect game" in a World Series. In game five of that series against the Brooklyn Dodgers, not a single Dodger reached a base on a hit, a walk, or an error!

As the game went into the ninth inning, the suspense mounted. The crowd of 64,519 cheered and waited. The last pitch was strike three. The side retired. The game was over. Perfect!

Mark the following statements either True (T), False (F), or Not Mentioned (N).

1. Don Larsen pitched a perfect game in a World Series. _____

2. Don Larsen's pitching record from 1953 to 1967 was not outstanding overall. _____

3. A crowd of 64,519 fans saw the only perfect World Series game ever. _____

4. The perfect game was the last in the series. _____

5. Don Larsen played for the Yankees. _____

Time/Sec.	3	5	7	10	12	15	17
WPM	2280	1368	977	684	570	456	402

Check your answers against the Appendix on page 152. If your time isn't shown, divide your time, in seconds, into 6840 for your WPM.

Reading #23

WHY PEOPLE SAY THEY READ

Why do people read? The amount of reading done by modern Americans is of great interest to some people. In today's TV-watching society, how much do people actually read? In most research being reported today, studies are concluding that approximately 90 percent of the Americans sampled say they have read a book or magazine within the last six months. That statistic varies from study to study, but one conclusion is rather obvious—an overwhelming majority of Americans read something more complicated than street signs and advertisements on billboards. The most common reason given by most people for reading was "general knowledge," followed closely by pleasure or leisure-recreation reading. Either third or fourth on most lists was "to obtain knowledge for work, job, or career." Thus, it is quite clear that most Americans (in spite of recent claims to the contrary) still spend a great deal of time reading; and their single most important reason for reading is to obtain general knowledge.

Mark the following statements either True (T), False (F), or Not Mentioned (N).

1. Most Americans no longer read much due to the amount of TV being watched. _____

2. Recent studies show a great majority of Americans do read. _____

3. The major reason cited by most people for reading is to obtain general knowledge rather than for leisure or relaxation. _____

4. Most people read to fulfill educational requirements. _____

5. The second most frequently cited reason for reading comes under the heading of leisure or relaxation. _____

Time/Sec.	4	6	8	10	12	15	20	25
WPM	2565	1710	1282	1026	855	684	513	410

If your time isn't shown, divide your time, in seconds, into 10,260 for your WPM, and record it in the chart on page 150.

Chapter 10

READING MACHINES

Are there other options, not discussed in this book, that you can try and that will improve your reading speed and comprehension? Obviously, the answer is yes, for no one book can possibly describe every step that can be used to improve one's reading skills. If there's a job to do, many people look to a machine to do it, and, yes, there are machines designed to help you read better and faster.

VIDEOCASSETTES AND
COMPUTER SOFTWARE PROGRAMS

The latest technology in reading machines designed to teach you how to speed read can be found in videocassettes and computer software packages—which have replaced the old reading programs on film. Obviously, the videocassettes and computer software programs are more user-friendly in that they are easier to use and more convenient, but the reading concepts presented are still the same. The message is still the same—only the manner in which it is delivered to the viewer is different. For example, eliminating regressions as a method of improving reading speed is the same message or concept today on a modern videocassette as it was years ago on film or centuries before that in ancient Greece.

The difference is you learn by reading messages displayed on a screen instead of reading print on paper. The eye movements people make are still the same: left to right, eye span, regressions, fixations, etc. People, however, are often fascinated by machines. Using this fascination or attraction as a form of motivation can be helpful if it induces the reader to practice and learn the speed reading steps. You can do the same things by applying the steps from this book to whatever words you read, whether they are on a screen or a printed page or even a highway sign.

Most people read more from printed pages in their daily lives than they do from a screen, so it is a good idea to master the concepts in the media in which you spend most of your time. The skills do transfer, however, from screen to print and vice versa. The key is to practice and master the steps, regardless of whether you use a reading machine or not.

The only caution I have for you about machines comes from years of teaching speed reading and using machines: Do not develop an over-reliance on the machines, whether they be electric or mechanical, to force your reading rate to accelerate to such an extent that, when you are not using the machines, your rate returns to its original status. The goal is to improve your reading rate and be able to keep it without any reliance upon periodic practice on a screen or machine.

TACHISTOSCOPE

Another reading machine, the tachistoscope, is like a camera shutter that opens and closes, allowing images (usually words or phrases) to be seen by the reader for fractions of a second. Thus, the reader is forced to read with little or no hesitation. The eye span must broaden so that the material may be read quickly. Fixations must be few and very short in duration. Subvocalizing is greatly reduced since one cannot say the words fast enough to keep up with the shutter as it opens and closes. The idea is that the reader will transfer the eye movements learned on the screen to the printed page.

The tachistoscope is a very old invention. Thousands of years ago the Greeks were concerned that they couldn't read their scrolls fast enough. They invented the tachistoscope, which in Greek means "swift viewing." The Greeks' tachistoscope was very much like the reading-window card shown in chapter 2. The Greeks, of course, didn't have camera shutters, so they used the reading-window card to increase their recognition rate so that they could see more words at one time as they read down the scroll. Their method was lost for many years. It enjoyed a slight revival around 1900, but it wasn't until the technological revolution of the World War II period that the concept of a tachistoscope was dusted off and revitalized.

Some combat pilots are still trained to recognize other aircraft by a technique similar to the tachistoscope or speedioscope. This is a process in which silhouettes of aircraft are flashed on a screen for a fraction of a second, and the pilots must accurately identify many kinds of aircraft. I have often had pilots, or former pilots, in speed-reading classes; it is amazing to see their average starting speed to be in the 300, 400, even 500 WPM range, largely because their eyes have been trained by hours of tachistoscopic training to move quickly and accurately. Their training in eye movements and quick recognition carries over into their reading.

Another interesting aspect of tachistoscopic training in recent years has been its newfound use by pro football teams. Some of them use the machine to train quarterbacks to see and identify more players more rapidly. The opposing linebackers sometimes key their defense off the quarterback's eye movements. Eye fixation patterns made by quarterbacks are easily detected by linemen. A regression as the quarterback scrambles in the backfield looking for a receiver is sometimes even noticeable to the TV viewer, as the ballplayer's head turns or his eyes sweep back. Some pro quarterbacks have spent hours on tachistoscopes training their eyes to make fewer fixations and still see more rapidly and accurately. Eye patterns of baseball players are important as well.

Tachistoscopes can be purchased at some stores carrying educational equipment. Many schools and universities have such machines available. Some public libraries also have this equipment available for readers to use at the library or to check out. There are slides made for all reading levels, from preschool to teenage to college to adult. In ordering a tachistoscope, one should specify the level of reading material to be included on the slides.

EYE-SPAN TRAINER

One version of the tachistoscope has recently taken on a new name; it is called an eye-span trainer, since that is its basic function. This small hand-held machine trains the eyes to move in a certain span: two, three, four, five, six, eight words at a time. The material is shown for controlled periods of time as brief as one-hundredth of a second. The slowest speed is usually one second. It isn't difficult to learn to see two or three words at a single glance before the shutter closes on the eye-span trainer. If your major concern is to improve and increase your eye span, you may want to consider using the eye-span trainer in conjunction with the theories presented in this book.

PACE-ACCELERATOR

The pacer, or accelerator, is a small table-top machine with a sloped platform on which you can place a book or magazine of your choice; thus, you can read whatever material you like. You then set the pacer at the desired rate of so many words per minute. Most pacers have a range of 200 to 2000 WPM. Pacers with a higher range, up to 10,000 WPM, are available but cost more. Some pacers I've seen come with a red light that goes on when a person is reading above 4000 WPM. For many readers that provides an incentive to hit a speed high enough to turn on the light.

In any event, the reading pacer works like this: You place your reading material under the machine and set the desired WPM. Then a barlike piece of metal or beam of light descends over the page while you are reading. The descending bar of light prevents regressing or re-reading. It is designed to force you to read at the desired rate, or WPM. You may accelerate or slow it down as you wish, depending on your abilities, the purpose, type of material being read, et. I have found this device especially good for reducing vocalizing or subvocalizing. It really pushes your recognition rate and can be ideal for forcing you to read in thought units or large groups of words. By setting the pacer faster and faster you may increase your reading rate as well as your ability to concentrate. It should be noted that both the eye-span trainer and pacer have been used to increase powers of concentration.

When I was in the Air Force, we were given a course in speed reading. The instructor set the WPM on the pacer higher and higher each day. It was difficult at first to keep up. I thought my comprehension was practically zero. I could catch glimpses of the material, but I was missing so much as the bar descended down each page at an even faster clip that I became rather frustrated. Once I no longer relied on reading every word and eliminated my regression habit, I began to pick up speed and comprehension. Then the instructor set the machine back from 1200 WPM to about 450 WPM. Suddenly, reading at 450 was a breeze, though it was something I couldn't do before I took that course. I had started at 200 WPM, so 450 with 80 percent comprehension seemed to me to be a remarkable accomplishment.

What I did not know then was that after the course was over, I would gradually go back to my original speed. The problem was I no longer had the machine to force me to read at 450 WPM. Without the periodic stimulation of the pacer, my reading speed gradually dropped back. So I took another course and began an intensive study on the subject of speed reading. This time the instructor explained what regressions were and thus I began to see what the pacer had done for me: It eliminated my regressions temporarily, but without the proper understanding of what my eyes were doing and how the reading process worked, I had slipped back to my old reading rate and begun regressing again. The new awareness and understanding of regressions and their effect on reading immediately shot my speed upward to newer, greater speeds. I didn't need to rely on a reading machine. Once I knew what to do— for example, eliminate regressions—my efforts to improve my reading shifted from mechanical instruments and devices to book-centered practicing. The two together (reading machines and book-centered practice) can aid the reader to achieve new heights in reading speed. Based on my experience, however, I prefer the book-centered approach.

Research studies are not conclusive as to the relative merits of one type of training versus the other. Neither book- nor machine-centered practice will produce the same results for everyone. Success depends upon many factors within each individual's reading style and reading needs. I have found over the years that for most people reading machines will provide initial stimulation to reach spectacular gains in a very short period of time. But the new rate is not lasting, and the individual's speed almost always quickly declines—sometimes as rapidly as it went up. I have concluded that this is because the reader does not truly understand the reading process (for example, regressions, eye span, etc.) and because he or she has not practiced long enough to change old reading habits into permanent new ones. What's more, since most reading is done without a machine, total reliance on mechanical devices is unrealistic. What usually happens with such machines is that the reader reads like a demon for ten to fifteen minutes a day while on the machine, but then for the rest of the day reads in the regular way, complete with regressions and all the old, slow habits.

Evidence clearly shows that book-centered practice, which is what this book is all about, is much more likely to result in steady and relatively permanent improvements in your reading speed and comprehension. There is no doubt that machines can help some people to read better and faster. However, using machines without understanding the concepts behind them greatly reduces their effectiveness. Machines work best when used in conjunction with book materials and mastery of the steps outlined in this book. A person should be leery of reliance on machines to improve his or her reading.

The acceleration and improvement of your reading is important. It is only through your own efforts that your reading will become better than ever. Because reading is a human process, the person who pushes a button on a machine and then sits back expecting that machine to improve his or her reading is bound to be disappointed. Even this book cannot do it for you. It takes individual effort to change your reading skills. Take small steps, work at them gradually, set definite goals, and follow a routine as shown by the examples in chapter 6. These are all part of the journey to better reading. You can't expect your reading to change by itself. Motivation and willpower, combined with the tips and know-how explained in this book, will unlock the powers of speed and comprehension for you. These techniques have worked for thousands of students I've taught over the years—from elementary-age students to senior citizens and Ph.D.s. And yet, I must tell you the most powerful force to change your reading style is you—*you,* yourself.

Try the following two paragraphs and remember—go for *speed . . . speed . . . speed.*

Reading #24

BICYCLING

One of the newest crazes to hit the modern American public is bicycling. From suburbia to the inner city, bicycle sales are booming. Bicycling seems to have an appeal to people of all ages. It has especially caught on with those who don't want to get into jogging but who still want to get their bodies in shape. Latest physiological research indicates runners and cyclists have much in common in the results obtained, such as good physical fitness, lean and tightened muscles, an air of exhilaration, pride of accomplishment, and mental alertness. Those who enjoy bicycling say it is simple, inexpensive, easy, natural, and never boring. Those who excel in the art of cycling say the secret is pace—the steady, rhythmic movement of the legs. They say it is acquired through practice and, once mastered, enables one to consistently cycle farther, longer, and more easily . . . and feel better.

Mark the following statements either True (T), False (F), or Not Mentioned (N).

1. Bicycling is one of the latest crazes in America. _____
2. Aerobics is just as good for your physical fitness as cycling. _____
3. Bicycling is expensive. _____
4. The results of cycling are similar to those of running or jogging. _____
5. The secret to the art of cycling is in the steady pace. _____

Time/Sec.	3	5	7	10	12	15	17	20
WPM	3060	1836	1311	918	765	612	540	459

If your time isn't shown, divide your time, in seconds, into 9180 for your exact WPM.

Reading #25

SAVE THE TREES

We hear a lot about endangered animal species. Well, quite possibly the world's forest lands could also be in danger of extinction. For all the years people have inhabited the earth, trees have been a source of fuel, building material, profit, and inspiration. Legends tell of Buddha and Joan of Arc meditating beneath trees; the Druids of ancient Britain worshipped trees; and trees even figure largely in the early tales of the Hindus and Hebrews. Now forests are threatened as never before in earth's history. Man himself is lessening his quality of life, for large wooded areas are vital to the quality of soil, air, and water. Man is simply cutting down the world's forests at an alarmingly accelerating rate. What is needed to offset this potential disaster is reforestation and proper management of today's resources. The delicate balance of nature and the ecological cycle is vitally important to the quality of human life for us as well as generations to come. Thus, "saving the trees" can be an important contribution from this generation to those that follow.

Mark the following statements either True (T), False (F), or Not Mentioned (N).

1. Trees in some parts of the world might be considered endangered species. _____
2. Trees have been a source of fuel, building material, and inspiration. _____
3. Trees play a vital role in the quality of air, soil, and water. _____
4 The quality of human life is dependent on the balance of nature. _____
5. What is needed to offset the devastation of forests is reforestation and management of resources. _____

Time/Sec.	3	5	7	10	12	15	20	25
WPM	3700	2220	1585	1110	925	740	555	444

If your time isn't shown, divide your time, in seconds, into 11,100 for your WPM.

Chapter 11

THE SUPER-READERS

By now you have learned, through the steps explained in this book, that you can greatly improve your reading speed and comprehension. The steps and concepts are actually quite easy because they build on existing basic reading skills used by everyone. The fact is that most people read one word at a time. By increasing their eye span to reading two or more words at one time, their speed significantly increases. By eliminating regressions, their speed increases even more. Add other more-efficient eye movements and the speed increases further. Comprehension improves as the brain perceives larger thought messages and these carry more interpretive meaning to the thinking-reading process in the brain. Speed reading isn't hard. It is really a question of how much improvement is desired by the reader.

After teaching these steps for many years to thousands of people, I have found that the concepts explained in this book are the easiest for most people to master—or to put it simply, most people can utilize these steps to improve their reading abilities, if they try. By using these methods and by practicing, people can go from 200 WPM to as high as 2000 WPM or more. I have even had students who read over 10,000 WPM. I have noticed that "super-readers"—those who read above 5000 WPM—used eye movements that were different from those of the speed readers in the 1200-WPM range.

In every human endeavor there are super-achievers, but the super-stars are usually few and far between. They certainly are not found in large numbers. Reading is no exception: There are few people who can read beyond 1500–2000 WPM.

How do these super-readers manage to read at 5000 or 8000 WPM? Did you ever see a speed-reading demonstration at which the reader glances at the page for 1 or 2 seconds, turns it . . . and repeats the process as he or she breezes through a chapter or book? How do such readers do it?

The answer is that they have honed their reading skills to a highly developed state with hours, days, and weeks of practice. Remember, these are the super-readers. Maybe you can be one of the speed-reading super-stars. I will show you how. It can be done, but it will take you more practice—a lot more. Most people taking a speed-reading course try to double their WPM. That's a common goal—to be twice as good as when you started the course. Most people would consider a 100 percent gain in personal self-improvement habits (like reading) to be a truly significant accomplishment. So going from 200 to 400 WPM is great. With much practice, a few people can go from 200 WPM to 5000 or 7000 WPM or higher. Here's how.

First, their eye patterns are not one or two or three words at one time. They do not read left to right, one word at a time, line after line. Do they skim or scan? No. Skimming is perusing each line looking for key words that give continuity of meaning without reading every word. Scanning is like glancing through a phone book looking for a certain name. Scanning is a form of speed-reading by finding then fixating on only a particular word or words. The reader really isn't reading all those other words.

The super-readers neither skim nor scan. Let's look at their eye movements. First, this type of reader begins to realize that his or her eye span can cover three or four words at a time out of a six to eight word line. This reader can see and read the entire line in two spans and one fixation:

The big red house is on Euclid Street.

Compare that to the reader seeing and reading one word at a time:

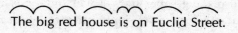

The big red house is on Euclid Street.

When we add a regression for this latter reader who is reading one word at a time, the reading pattern looks like this:

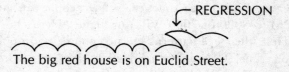

The big red house is on Euclid Street.

Which of these reading patterns would be faster? The first eye pattern, with two scans and one fixation per line, is probably ten times faster than reading one word at a time, and this faster reader doesn't even miss any words. In fact, the first

reading pattern offers a better chance for comprehension because it takes in large clusters or words that make more sense
or have more meaning when grouped together than they do
singly. For example:

The big red house   2 thought units
is on Euclid Street.   in 2 eye jumps
                                     = 2 ideas or
                                       2 messages of thought
                                       to the reader.

From reading two or three or four words at one time, the
reader can, with some time and practice, train his or her eye
movements to cover an entire line at one time. These entire
line-movements can be readily developed on the narrow columns found in newspapers and most magazines. The reader's
eye movement would look like this:

America is on the rebound. The "decline school of thought" starting in the late 1960s or early 1970s is giving way to a new sense of self-confidence in America and the American way of life. Perhaps never before in the history of any government or nation have so many governments become democratic, in emulation of the U.S. form of government.

Lou Harris, the famous pollster, first picked up signs of lagging confidence in the late 1960s, and the 1970s were no better. The 1980s were further stampeded by an ever-growing Japanese industrial might.

However, recent events in the national scene have stemmed the tide in favor of a returning sense of strength and confidence in America.

An inferiority complex is always tough to overcome. Belief in one's self and in America go hand in hand. It is good to see America on the rebound!

As you can see by examining the number of words this reader above is reading, he or she is covering as many as eight words in a single glance with no regressions and only one fixation per line. Compare that with the reader on page 122 who reads one word at a time with regressions and ten fixations per line. Eye patterns make the difference in speed—not IQ or vocabulary.

The reader covering an entire line at one time can, with time and practice, read two or three lines with one eye span. Such reading would look like this:

America is on the rebound. The "decline school of thought" starting in the late 1960s or early 1970s is giving way to a new sense of self-confidence in America and the American way of life. Perhaps never before in the history of any government or nation have so many governments become democratic, in emulation of the U.S. form of government.

Lou Harris, the famous pollster, first picked up signs of lagging confidence in the late 1960s, and the 1970s were no better. The 1980s were further stampeded by an ever growing Japanese industrial might.

However, recent events in the national scene have stemmed the tide in favor of a returning sense of strength and confidence in America.

An inferiority complex is always tough to overcome. Belief in one's self and in America go hand in hand. It is good to see America on the rebound!

From two or three lines at one time, the reader can read "zigzag" down the page like this:

America is on the rebound. The "decline school of thought" starting in the late 1960s or early 1970s is giving way to a new sense of self-confidence in America and the American way of life. Perhaps never before in the history of any government or nation have so many governments become democratic, in emulation of the U.S. form of government.

Lou Harris, the famous pollster, first picked up signs of lagging confidence in the late 1960s, and the 1970s were no better. The 1980s were further stampeded by an ever growing Japanese industrial might.

However, recent events in the national scene have stemmed the tide in favor of a returning sense of strength and confidence in America.

An inferiority complex is always tough to overcome. Belief in one's self and in America go hand in hand. It is good to see America on the rebound!

After this diagonal zigzag technique is mastered, one can develop "vertical" reading eye patterns where an entire paragraph is read at one glance or one fixation like this:

America is on the rebound. The "decline school of thought" starting in the late 1960s or early 1970s is giving way to a new sense of self-confidence in America and the American way of life. Perhaps never before in the history of any government or nation have so many governments become democratic, in emulation of the U.S. form of government.

Lou Harris, the famous pollster, first picked up signs of lagging confidence in the late 1960s, and the 1970s were no better. The 1980s were further stampeded by an ever growing Japanese industrial might.

However, recent events in the national scene have stemmed the tide in favor of a returning sense of strength and confidence in America.

An inferiority complex is always tough to overcome. Belief in one's self and in America go hand in hand. It is good to see America on the rebound!

How many people can achieve super speeds? Not many, but this is the way they learn to do it. Once shown, it becomes largely a matter of motivation, need, and practice—lots of practice.

Magazines that are easy to read—especially those with columns approximately $1^{5}/_{8}''$ wide—are ideal for practicing this type of zigzag or vertical speed reading or even targeting paragraphs. Try it on the following sample paragraphs and see. When trying these new eye patterns, don't be concerned about comprehension at first. The idea is to discover how the eyes can move in different patterns and how amazingly high reading speeds can be achieved by using these different eye patterns.

Picture this: One
partner in a dating
couple gets invited
to play softball on a
Saturday afternoon,
and the other partner
responds, "Go on,
Honey, have a good
time."

　If you assumed the guy
played ball while the
girl played martyr,
your stereotypes may
need some updating.
In today's changing
times, sexual stereo-
types are rapidly
changing. In dating
relationships, today's
couples think it is
socially acceptable to
be involved in activities
that exclude a lover or
a spouse, such as
devoting time to a hobby,
going out with a friend,
or spending time alone.

Try another:

Notice the narrow columns.

These are ideal to develop
zigzag and vertical eye
movements.

You're frantically trying to
make that 8 A.M. deadline,
and it happens again: Your
stomach churns, your head
throbs and your face looks

like a war zone. You know
you're able to handle the
pressure. So why is your
body turning traitor?

Researchers have deter-
mined that hormones re-
leased by the brain during
high-stress jags can trigger
health woes in both men and
women. However, a wom-
an's more complicated hor-
monal structure may make
her more prone to physical
flare-ups. But by recognizing
work-stress symptoms, you
can help keep yourself
healthy *and* get the job done.

Most people do not need to achieve super speeds, and most
people won't practice enough to develop their skills to such
exceptional levels. Most people can, however, greatly improve
their reading and speed read by using the basic concepts, skills,
and exercises as presented in this book. Given a reasonable
amount of time and effort, these reading skills can be developed
by most people. Speed-reading secrets are not geared to IQ,
vocabulary, or material. Speed reading is basically geared to
eye movement proficiency, which is changed and developed after practicing the new techniques.

Reading is an individual activity that is influenced by many
factors, among them the material to be read, the purpose for
reading, vocabulary, reading speed, and comprehension. Develop reading styles and skills that are comfortable for you.
Happy reading!

Chapter 12

READING HABITS OF SOME FAMOUS AMERICANS

It is interesting to consider the reading patterns of some famous Americans, past and present, whose positions have required them to read vast amounts of material. Perhaps we can gain insights into reading methods from some of these well-known Americans.

GEORGE WASHINGTON

It is said that Washington liked to read even when he was on horseback. He would move his lips to form the passages he was reading and "hear the words with his inner ear," as they referred to this process back then. His reading speed was not so ferocious as was his appetite to read everything he could put his hands on. He especially liked English books on agriculture, because he considered himself a country gentleman farmer. He had a steady, consistent rate and paced himself through material without a lot of backing up and re-reading. Occasionally, however, historical narratives state that he would re-read an entire page or a whole chapter.

THOMAS JEFFERSON

Jefferson believed in mapping out his reading into a definite plan of action, covering each topic with a particular purpose and never allowing himself to deviate from his reading schedule until it had been fully carried out. No distractions, no dissipation of time by scattered inattentiveness—these are the keys to understanding Jefferson's tremendous power of concentration. He believed that one should choose a course of reading very purposefully for definite needed knowledge, cultivation, or recreation. He would make lists of books in various categories to be read.

Jefferson used a clock to schedule himself precisely and always recommended "knowing where you are, and what you are doing, and what time it is, and whether you are falling short of your schedule or not, and how far short." It is clear that this was what he made himself do in all matters, and particularly in his reading. We know that constant deliberate eye movements tend to increase speed and prevent dawdling. Jefferson's speed was "always calm, even stately, like the tick of a tall mahogany clock." But it was fast, nevertheless, with no false steps or jerks of uncertainly. His progress was massive and real.

ABRAHAM LINCOLN

The story of Abraham Lincoln's educating himself by candlelight has become an integral part of American folk legend. Lincoln begged or borrowed every book in sight. He was an avid reader. In his early youth there was very little chance for him to obtain any broad, cosmopolitan reading material. Later he studied his law books in great detail, often reading and re-reading words and whole lines over and over again. He would use his self-taught reading habits in his career as a lawyer, legislator, and president. It is said that, for Lincoln, reading was a relief from the constant, harrowing anxiety he often experienced during the Civil War. He liked reading Shakespeare's *Richard II* aloud to his family in the White House. He knew that, in the midst of those sad, turbulent days, he could turn to the literature he loved for refreshment. He read aloud (even to himself) because he liked to hear the words and thus feel renewed after long hours of hard work as president.

THEODORE ROOSEVELT

Teddy Roosevelt was a tireless reviewer of books and a very rapid reader. He was the "colonel of the Rough Riders" in speed reading. The amount he could read at one time would seem incredible if he had not left us valuable hints as to his style and methods of covering massive amounts of reading material. He never said in exact numbers just how fast he could read or how his rates differed on different sorts of books, but we can easily infer that he sometimes skipped and scanned materials and varied the rate according to his purpose. On this point we have a delightful series of letters to his son Kermit about how he read Dickens: "It always interests me about Dickens to think how almost all of it was mixed up with every kind of cheap, second-rate matter. . . . The wise thing to do is simply to skip the bosh and twaddle and vulgarity and untruth, and get the benefit out of the rest." Note that this advice to skip and scan and vary the rate comes from a lover of Dickens, a wise, discriminating reader, who could treasure the best.

Roosevelt liked to read certain books repeatedly. In fact, he has left a list of novels that he read not only once but "over and over again": *Guy Mannering, The Antiquary, Pendennis, Vanity Fair, Our Mutual Friend,* and *Pickwick Papers.* Roosevelt has also told us that he would judge the contents of a book from the index, the table of contents, or the chapter headings, all of which indicate what subject matter is included.

The most important thing to notice about Roosevelt's reading, however, is not his enormous range of materials so much as his free use of a whole gamut of methods for different reading purposes. He would use his fingers to pace himself through a book, read parts of it slowly, skip boldly over other parts, read at a prodigious rate of speed, read carefully for review, and read some stories over and over again. And he read at a flexible rate: slow or fast, depending on his need.

FRANKLIN D. ROOSEVELT

FDR was probably among America's super-readers of all time. He could read an entire paragraph at a single glance! He started out like everyone else—reading one, then two words at a time. He increased that to three and four words. Soon he could read six and eight words in a single eye span. After that, it wasn't long before he could read an entire line at one glance. Not satisfied, he practiced reading two lines at a time—with a single eye movement. Then he began to zigzag his way down the page, reading half a paragraph with one eye movement. Just two or three eye jumps and the entire page was finished! He would quickly run his eyes down the page, then turn the page, reading to digest the author's thoughts. Thumbing through a book at one sitting wasn't unusual for FDR.

JOHN F. KENNEDY

JFK became an extremely fast reader after he took a course in speed reading. It is reported that his reading speed was approximately 284 WPM before he studied speed reading, but he worked at it until he reached a speed of about 1200 WPM. His great range of speed allowed him much flexibility to vary the rate on material as he saw fit. He often liked to use rapid eye-span movements to pick up key words and important phrases. He also liked to read in large groups of thought units. However, the real strength in his reading repertoire was his ability to use varying rates of speed for the numerous types of reading materials that came across his desk.

CONTEMPORARY TV PERSONALITIES

With the amount of TV viewing done by people today, most viewers have become familiar with the cue cards held by the studio crew so that the stars don't forget their lines. Cue cards are also used to give TV personalities messages like "cut" or "Time for a commercial." When audiences see stars stumble over words on the cue cards, they find this reading process amusing because they identify with it. They either go through it themselves or have seen other readers do so, but it is especially funny to see it on TV, where usually we see the very best in sports and entertainment. We expect TV super-stars to be super in everything they do, including reading, and when we see them make the same little human errors we all do, it makes us laugh and identify with them even more.

TV newscasters Dan Rather, Tom Brokaw, and Peter Jennings are familiar to millions of Americans. To a trained observer, the eye movements of these celebrities are readily distinguishable as they read news from the prepared reports held in front of them. Their eye-span movements are excellent.

They read in large groups of thought units and speak in a style that makes their news announcements very easy to understand. Listen to their next news reports and see for yourself. I have never seen them use any motor movements to read, and they very seldom regress. You don't see them fixate on words for long. Their reading rates also appear to be far above average. All of these factors contribute to their success in reading and presenting the nightly news reports.

Late-night host Johnny Carson reads cue cards very well, and when he does regress or misread or fixate for long on a word, he jokes about it. The audience laughs with him, too. Regis Philbin's reading speed is a bit slower; he makes more regressions and fixations. Larry King, on the other hand, has a reading style comprised of exceptionally large, quick eye spans; fixations are few, and regressions are practically non-existent.

The reading habits of famous Americans can be documented from the present all the way back to George Washington. It's interesting to see how the rich and famous have reading patterns or styles similar to those found in everyone else. It's also inspiring to see how some of the rich and famous have adapted their reading skills to amazing speeds and styles.

Chapter 13

PRACTICE EXERCISES

The following exercises are provided to give you additional opportunities to continue mastering your newfound reading skills. The Progress Chart in the back has been designed so that you can continue to keep a record of your development. In any program of self-improvement, systematic practice over an extended period of time is most effective.

Time works on your side. Try to keep a certain amount of time set aside each day for practice. Apply yourself wholeheartedly and watch your progress. See and feel your success! After practicing, try several of these readings and quizzes each day. (See pages 151–152 for answers.)

Watch your progress continue. From time to time you may want to refer back to this book for a few refreshing tips and even re-read some of these practice exercises, just to see how you are doing. You'll be amazed how you have corrected your old reading weaknesses and learned new reading skills!

Reading #26

A DIAMOND IS FOREVER

It starts with a diamond . . . and a promise to share their lives together . . . forever. That's when forever doesn't seem long enough for two people who are in love and want to spend the rest of their lives together. They promise to always be sensitive to each other's needs. And even after they're married, to always be there . . . sometimes just to listen. They promise to always be honest with each other and bring things out in the open where they can talk them over. They promise to share . . . and that's the part of their love they don't ever want to lose. A diamond is their promise to each other that they never will.

Mark the following statements either True (T), False (F), or Not Mentioned (N).

1. A diamond is forever. _____
2. A diamond is a promise they will always share and love each other. _____
3. Diamonds hold their value, and therefore are good investments. _____
4. Sometimes people want someone there just to listen. _____
5. For two people in love, forever doesn't seem long enough. _____

Time/Sec.	2	4	6	8	10	12	15
WPM	3570	1785	1190	892	714	595	476

If your time isn't shown, divide your time, in seconds, into 7140 for your WPM.

Reading #27

BETTER READING = MORE INCOME

A better job with higher pay may actually result from one's ability to read and obtain more education. In this age of speed, the person who can do more work in less time usually is rewarded by increased income or more leisure time. Most of us are interested in such benefits, and thus the number of people who spend time and money to improve their reading is increasing daily. Since most of us can double or triple our reading efficiency, the gains we might derive from such self-improvement can be great indeed. You might then say that better reading equals more income.

Mark the following statements either True (T), False (F), or Not Mentioned (N).

1. The number of people spending time and money to improve their reading is decreasing every day. _____
2. Most of us can double or triple our reading efficiency. _____
3. More leisure time can result from better reading. _____
4. Schools should teach these speed-reading techniques. _____
5. Better reading equals more income. _____

Time/Sec.	2	4	6	8	10	12	15
WPM	3330	1665	1110	832	666	555	444

If your time isn't shown, divide your time, in seconds, into 6660 for your WPM. Don't forget to keep track of your continued improvement by using the Progress Chart in the back of the book.

You might find it interesting to compare your reading speed and comprehension scores at this stage to those you achieved for Reading #1. The results will show you how much progress you've made and how much better and faster you can now read as a result of using the tips and techniques found in this book.

Reading #28

HALLOWEEN

Halloween isn't the same anymore! Remember when you could cut two holes in a sheet to be a ghost or just rummage through Mom and Dad's old stuff for that ultimate Halloween outfit?

Halloween today looks like a Broadway show, complete with a wide range of costumes from serious to silly, from TV characters to classic creatures and monsters.

Costumes like Frankenstein, circus clowns, devils, witches, and bunnies are good ol' fashioned standbys that can still be seen, but new ones like Ninja warriors and rock stars are big hits for today's grade schoolers. There are even baby costumes for toddlers that are mini versions of what big brothers or sisters are wearing. Fun? Today's kids enjoy Halloween as much as we did. Halloween is always a fun time for trick or treaters.

Mark the following statements either True (T), False (F), or Not Mentioned (N).

1. Halloween isn't the same anymore. _____
2. Costumes are more diversified and far ranging, from serious to silly. _____
3. Some costumes are still good ol' standbys. _____
4. There are even baby costumes today. _____
5. Halloween is a national holiday. _____

Time/Sec.	2	4	6	8	10	12	15	17
WPM	3975	1987	1325	994	795	662	530	467

If your time isn't shown, divide your time, in seconds, into 7950 for your WPM.

Reading #29

MAKING A GOOD FIRST IMPRESSION

How people regard you intially can mean warm or cold feelings later on, for first impressions are often lasting impressions. First encounters or initial impressions are key factors that can determine success or failure in those critical moments such as job interviews, sales presentations, business luncheons, or meeting his/her parents for the first time. There are some rules that, if followed, will help you create a positive image for yourself during those initial encounters. The first and most obvious impression is created by the way you dress. You should dress the way you want to be perceived. Second: Do your homework before you meet new people. Know a little about them. They'll be flattered you took the time, and it'll give you a basis for conversation. Next: Don't be late. Show that you respect their time. It's as valuable as yours. Fourth: Get the name and periodically use it in the conversation. Fifth and last: Listen. Don't dominate the conversation, and don't be the silent nonparticipant either. A good listener is still involved in the conversation. If you follow these rules, you'll make the first impression a good one!

Mark the following statements either True (T), False (F), or Not Mentioned (N).

1. First impressions are often lasting impressions. _____
2. Good talkers are good listeners. _____

3. The way you dress creates first impressions. _____
4. First encounters are key factors that can determine success or failure. _____
5. Being polite and courteous is another factor involved in first impressions. _____

Time/Sec.	3	5	7	10	12	15	17	20	25
WPM	4100	2460	1757	1230	1025	820	723	615	492

If your time isn't shown, divide your time, in seconds, into 12,300 for your WPM.

Reading #30

FEEDING THE BIRDS

The joy of attracting birds is open to everyone and is remarkably easy if certain basic guidelines are followed. Birds need food, water, shelter from predators, and places to raise their young. Provide birds with the kind of food they like and with nearby trees, shrubs, or flowers that create a natural habitat for shelter and wild birds will flock to your property. The most important aspect of setting up a successful bird feeding station is, of course, to provide the kind of food they like. The number one food choice of most song birds is the sunflower seed. Be patient when you first put out a new feeder. The birds will soon arrive.

Answer the following questions either True (T), False (F), or Not Mentioned (N).

1. Feeding the birds is remarkably easy. _____
2. The redbird or Cardinal is the most popular bird. _____
3. The most important aspect of attracting birds to our property is providing the kind of food they like. _____

4. The choice food of most songbirds is the sunflower seed. _____

5. The type of feeder you place and its location are critical factors in attracting birds. _____

Time/Sec.	2	3	4	5	7	10	12
WPM	3540	2360	1770	1418	1011	708	590

If your time isn't shown, divide your time, in seconds, into 7080 for your WPM.

Reading #31

MONTICELLO

Monticello was Thomas Jefferson's mountaintop plantation. If places can be said to shape destinies, then Monticello was such a place, for it was at the very heart of Jefferson's visionary genius. Monticello was his inspiration and his retreat. It was his place for reflection and thinking. Long before he wrote the Declaration of Independence or held the governorship of Virginia or the presidency of the United States, or founded the University of Virginia, his mountaintop retreat held his dreams and efforts. The house was begun in 1769 when he was a young lawyer of twenty-six. The house was continually in a state of remodeling and expansion. The major construction was concluded in 1809 but continued until his death at the age of eighty-three on July 4th, 1826—a span of some fifty-seven years his mountaintop home was the object of his genius. Today Monticello still reveals the brilliance and versatility of one of America's extraordinarily bright minds.

Answer the following questions either True (T), False (F), or Not Mentioned (N).

1. Monticello is close to Mt. Vernon, the home of another famous American president. _____
2. Monticello is located in the tidewater part of Virginia. _____
3. Jefferson worked on Monticello for some fifty-seven years, right up to the time of his death. _____
4. The major construction of the plantation home was completed in 1809. _____
5. Monticello means mountaintop. _____

Time/Sec.	2	3	4	5	7
WPM	4830	3220	2415	1932	1380

If your time isn't shown, divide your time, in seconds, into 9660 for your WPM.

Reading #32

SMARTER CARS TO COME

With the blossoming of electronics, cars are rapidly changing. "Smart car" technology is almost here. By 2000, much of the following electronic technology will be standard on cars due to the computer age. Suspension, or the car's ride, will instantly change from luxury sedan to sports car at the flick of a switch by the driver. Traction control on slippery roads will be done by a computer that senses when a wheel is spinning too fast and slows it down so the tire will grip the road. Radar detection may be coupled with radar cruise control that may slow the car down automatically. Navigation systems will be on-board video screens showing maps, your location, routes to follow, and even alternate routes around obstacles. Self-tinting glass will be similar to the sun glasses that darken or lighten according to light density. Head-up displays adapted from aircraft will give you more information than you ever wanted to know about your car. You won't have to take your eyes off the road either, because the readings will appear out in front of the car.

These electronic computer-driver "car smarts" will be in addition to today's electronics, such as cruise control, service requirements, engine statistics, power seats, windows, door locks, transmissions, pollution control, brakes. All the electronics will be managed through a master on-board computer, which will coordinate the operation of the car for maximum efficiency. While the air bag and anti-lock brakes may be new to American cars this year, the cars of tomorrow will see an ever-increasing array of computer technology.

Mark the following statements either True (T), False (F), or Not Mentioned (N).

1. By the year 2000, computer smart cars will be a reality.
   _____

2. General Motors and Chrysler Corporation are combining resources to bring electronic improvements to auto technology.
   _____

3. On-board video screens will be able to show you your location and route to your destination. _____

4. Technology in auto electronics is lead by the Japanese.
   _____

5. Lee Iacocca, head of Chrysler, foresees electronic technology as standard equipment on cars of the future. _____

Time/Sec.	5	7	10	12	15	17	20	25	30
WPM	3180	2271	1590	1325	1060	935	795	636	530

If your time isn't shown, divide your time, in seconds, into 15,900 for your WPM.

Reading #33

WHAT'S NEW AT THE SUPERMARKET?

Many grocery chains now hire full-fledged chefs to plan and oversee their prepared-food sections. Grocery stores today can offer everything from fresh stuffed chicken breasts, marinated steaks, and upscale salads, to fresh flowers, handmade chocolates, and carry-out entrees so tasty that many consumers consider these new stores as complete one-stop facilities for home entertaining.

Is anyone in the kitchen anymore? People who say the end of home cooking is in sight or soon to be here might want to talk to cooks who say that they still enjoy being home at the range on some days or that they purchase some prepared items at these new grocery stores so they can concentrate on special desserts or gourmet dishes. Homestyle or carry-out? It's all part of today's changing American life-styles.

Mark the following sentences either True (T), False (F), or Not Mentioned (N).

1. Supermarkets are changing places. _____
2. Gourmet foods can be purchased at some new supermarkets. _____
3. The range of already prepared foods that can be purchased in today's supermarket is significant. _____
4. Some people think home cooking is rapidly becoming a thing of the past. _____
5. The cost of already prepared foods at today's supermarket is most reasonable. _____

Time/Sec.	2	3	5	7	10	12	15	17
WPM	3960	2640	1584	1131	792	660	528	466

If your time isn't shown, divide your time, in seconds, into 7920 for your WPM.

Reading #34

THE 1927 NEW YORK YANKEES

The New York Yankees have won 22 World Series champion-ships, more than any other team. They have had many great teams, but the 1927 Yankees may have been the best team of all time. The Yankees won 110 games and lost only 44 that season.

That 1927 team had many powerful hitters, led by Babe Ruth and Lou Gehrig. Ruth hit 60 homes runs that season. No other team hit more than 56 that year. Gehrig was equally impressive with 47 homers and a .373 batting average. He set a major league record of 175 runs batted in.

The Yankees beat the Pittsburgh Pirates in the World Series that year four games to none. Ruth hit two home runs in four games. The Yankees of 1927 rank as one of baseball's greatest teams of all time.

Mark the following sentences either True (T), False (F), or Not Mentioned (N).

1. The New York Yankees have won 22 World Series Champi-onships, more than any other team. _____
2. The 1927 New York Yankees was one of the all-time great baseball teams. _____
3. The Cleveland Indians won the 1948 World Series. _____
4. Babe Ruth hit 60 home runs in 1927. _____
5. Lou Gehrig, one of baseball's greats, was a member of the 1927 New York Yankees team. _____

Time/Sec.	2	3	5	7	10	12	15	17
WPM	4230	2820	1692	1208	846	705	564	498

If your time isn't shown above, divide your time, in seconds, into 8460 for your WPM.

Reading #35

CHRISTOPHER COLUMBUS— MASTER NAVIGATOR

Christopher Columbus was a master navigator in a far-off age. In a few years, in 1992, it will be the 500th anniversary of the ocean voyage of this remarkable Italian mariner, navigator, and astronomer. Columbus sailed the seas many years before the sextant was invented. There was no science of navigation and no method of finding a ship's position on the open seas. The best instrument he had was crude and imprecise. Columbus used a quadrant, a quarter of a circle that could be used to measure the changes in altitude of the sun, moon, and stars.

Columbus was able to keep tracking his approximate position throughout the long voyage across the vast ocean and back again to Spain. Columbus discovered facts that were hard for people of those days to accept.

Mark the following statements either True (T), False (F), or Not Mentioned (N).

1. Christopher Columbus was a master mariner, navigator, and astronomer. _____
2. He sailed the seas to America in 1492. _____
3. Columbus was one of America's famous astronauts. _____
4. Magellan sailed the oceans along with Columbus. _____

5. Columbus was unable to navigate by measuring changes in
   the altitude of the sun, moon, and stars. _____

Time/Sec.	2	3	5	7	10	12	15	17
WPM	4080	2720	1632	1165	816	680	544	480

If your time isn't shown, divide your time, in seconds, into
8160 for your WPM.

Appendix A:

PROGRESS CHART

	TIME (SEC.)	SPEED (WPM)	COMPREHENSION
Reading # 1	38.5	183.8	
Reading # 2			
Reading # 3			
Reading # 4			
Reading # 5			
Reading # 6			
Reading # 7			
Reading # 8			
Reading # 9			
Reading #10			
Reading #11			
Reading #12			
Reading #13			
Reading #14			
Reading #15			
Reading #16			
Reading #17			
Reading #18			
Reading #19			
Reading #20			
Reading #21			
Reading #22			

	TIME (SEC.)	SPEED (WPM)	COMPREHENSION
Reading #23			
Reading #24			
Reading #25			
Reading #26			
Reading #27			
Reading #28			
Reading #29			
Reading #30			
Reading #31			
Reading #32			
Reading #33			
Reading #34			
Reading #35			

Appendix B:

ANSWERS TO READING EXERCISES

EXAMPLES			ANSWERS		
1	1. T	2. F	3. T	4. T	5. F
2	1. F	2. N	3. N	4. T	5. T
3	1. T	2. N	3. T	4. F	5. T
4	1. T	2. F	3. N	4. T	5. N
5	1. T	2. T	3. N	4. N	5. F
6	1. T	2. N	3. T	4. F	5. T
7	1. F	2. T	3. F	4. N	5. F
8	1. N	2. N	3. T	4. T	5. F
9	1. T	2. T	3. N	4. T	5. T
10	1. T	2. N	3. T	4. F	5. F
11	1. T	2. F	3. N	4. T	5. N
12	1. T	2. F	3. N	4. N	5. T
13	1. F	2. T	3. F	4. N	5. T
14	1. T	2. T	3. F	4. F	5. T
15	1. N	2. T	3. T	4. N	5. T
16	1. T	2. F	3. T	4. N	5. N
17	1. N	2. N	3. T	4. T	5. N
18	1. T	2. T	3. T	4. T	5. N
19	1. T	2. N	3. T	4. N	5. T
20	1. T	2. F	3. T	4. N	5. T
21	1. T	2. T	3. T	4. T	5. F

EXAMPLES   **ANSWERS**

22	1. T	2. T	3. T	4. N	5. N
23	1. N	2. T	3. F	4. F	5. T
24	1. T	2. N	3. N	4. T	5. T
25	1. T	2. T	3. T	4. T	5. T
26	1. T	2. T	3. N	4. T	5. T
27	1. F	2. T	3. N	4. N	5. T
28	1. T	2. T	3. T	4. T	5. N
29	1. T	2. N	3. T	4. T	5. T
30	1. T	2. F	3. T	4. T	5. N
31	1. T	2. T	3. T	4. T	5. N
32	1. T	2. N	3. T	4. N	5. N
33	1. T	2. T	3. T	4. T	5. N
34	1. T	2. T	3. N	4. T	5. T
35	1. T	2. T	3. N	4. N	5 T

FINAL READING CHECKLIST

✓ GOOD EYE SPAN!

✓ NO REGRESSIONS!

✓ VARY THE RATE!

✓ NO SUBVOCALIZING!

✓ PRACTICE!

✓ GOOD RECOGNITION RATE!

✓ REDUCE FIXATIONS!

✓ READ WITH A PURPOSE!

✓ KEEP AT IT!

✓ ENJOY READING!

Speed Reading (2nd edition)
by Robert L. Zorn, Ph.D.

Since publication of the first edition in 1980, *Speed Reading* has helped thousands of readers improve their reading speed, comprehension, and enjoyment. With a consistent emphasis on how the eyes move across and down the page, Robert L. Zorn presents a simple and painless method for readers to double or even triple their reading speeds.

Dr. Zorn first discusses common habits that slow down the reading process: regression, the habit of re-reading one or more words per line; moving the body while reading; "hearing" the words that are read. He then introduces the key concept of "eye span"—the number of words taken in by the eye in one sweeping movement—and continues with specific techniques that enhance efficient eye span.

Entire chapters are devoted to word recognition and to comprehension and retention of what is read. Dr. Zorn describes and evaluates several "reading machines," and includes a discussion, which is new to this edition, of how to become a "super-reader" who can read 4,000 or 5,000 words per minute.

The book contains 35 specially designed passages for the reader's use in practicing speed-reading techniques. Each is accompanied by a simple comprehension quiz and a chart for determining reading speed. Dr. Zorn also explains how to calculate reading speed for any material.

INDEX

Abraham Lincoln, reading
    habits of, 131–32
Answers, to reading exercises,
    151–52
Association
  improving your
      comprehension and,
      86–87
  reading power and, 97
Attention
  improving your
      comprehension and, 84
  reading power and, 97
Auditory readers
  reading environments for, 24–
    25
  types of, 21–23
Auditory reading
  compared to sight reading,
    24–25
  result of phonics method of
    learning, 23–25
Average reading rates
  for adults, 4–5
  for different educational
    levels, 5

Background noise, reading with,
    25
Bad reading habits. *See under*
    Habits, reading
Body movement habit
  to correct, 20
  effect on comprehension, 19–
    20

Caution signals, 78
Children
  developing reading rate in,
    101
  recognition rate in, 72
Column width, effect on speed
    reading, 39
Comprehension
  body movement habit and,
    19–20
  eye-span method and, 33, 35,
    42–43
  improving your
    association and, 86–87
    attention and, 84
    concentration and, 85–86
    distributed practice and, 87